OCT 2 5 2010

1st EDITION

Perspectives on Modern World History

9/11

1st EDITION

Perspectives on Modern World History

9/11

Louise I. Gerdes

Editor

GREENHAVEN PRESS
A part of Gale, Cengage Learning

GALE
CENGAGE Learning™

Detroit • New York • San Francisco • New Haven, Conn • Waterville, Maine • London

W

GALE
CENGAGE Learning

Christine Nasso, *Publisher*
Elizabeth Des Chenes, *Managing Editor*

© 2010 Greenhaven Press, a part of Gale, Cengage Learning.

Gale and Greenhaven Press are registered trademarks used herein under license.

For more information, contact:
Greenhaven Press
27500 Drake Rd.
Farmington Hills, MI 48331-3535
Or you can visit our Internet site at gale.cengage.com

For product information and technology assistance, contact us at
Gale Customer Support, 1-800-877-4253.

For permission to use material from this text or product, submit all requests online at
www.cengage.com/permissions.

Further permissions questions can be e-mailed to permissionrequest@cengage.com

Articles in Greenhaven Press anthologies are often edited for length to meet page requirements. In addition, original titles of these works are changed to clearly present the main thesis and to explicitly indicate the author's opinion. Every effort is made to ensure that Greenhaven Press accurately reflects the original intent of the authors. Every effort has been made to trace the owners of copyrighted material.

Cover images © Alan Schein Photography/Corbis, © Neville Elder/Corbis Sygma.

LIBRARY OF CONGRESS CATALOGING-IN-PUBLICATION DATA
9/11 / Louise I. Gerdes, book editor.
     p. cm. -- (Perspectives on modern world history)
     Includes bibliographical references and index.
     ISBN 978-0-7377-4793-5 (hardcover)
  1. September 11 Terrorist Attacks, 2001--Influence. 2. War on Terrorism, 2001-2009.
     3. United States--Politics and government--2001-2009. I. Gerdes, Louise I., 1953- II.
     Title: Nine/eleven.
     HV6432.7.A105 2010
     973.931--dc22   2010000264

Printed in the United States of America
1 2 3 4 5 6 7 14 13 12 11 10

CONTENTS

CHAPTER 1   The Events and Aftermath of 9/11

   David Greenberg

   On September 11, 2001, 2,819 people died
   when terrorists crashed two planes into the
   World Trade Center in New York City and one
   plane into the Pentagon in Washington, DC.
   Passengers overcame the hijackers of a fourth
   plane that crashed in Pennsylvania. A Rutgers
   University history professor discusses the
   impact of and the response to the devastating
   destruction of these shocking attacks.

   Peter Finn

   Based on interviews with the family, friends,
   and associates of the Hamburg cell, a U.S.
   journalist in Berlin explores the milieu in
   Hamburg, Germany, that nurtured seven fun-
   damentalist Muslims with a shared hatred of
   the United States. Over two and a half years,
   key 9/11 terrorists lived in the open while
   developing their plan in secret.

security. He declares war against terrorism and any nation that harbors terrorists. In addition, he acknowledges U.S. courage and asks Americans to be patient and continue to uphold U.S. values.

CHAPTER 2   The Controversies Surrounding 9/11

American-Islamic Relations. The excess and materialism promoted by Hollywood and U.S. foreign policies that support the oppression of disenfranchised Muslims do, however, create the discontent that can lead to terrorism.

enacted laws that threaten civil liberties. These laws make it easier for law enforcement to access personal information, conduct surveillance, and search and seize personal property.

FOREWORD

*"History cannot give us a program for the future,
but it can give us a fuller understanding of ourselves, and of our common humanity, so that we
can better face the future."*
                                    —Robert Penn Warren,
                                    American poet and novelist

The history of each nation is punctuated by momentous events that represent turning points for that
nation, with an impact felt far beyond its borders.
These events—displaying the full range of human capabilities, from violence, greed, and ignorance to heroism,
courage, and strength—are nearly always complicated
and multifaceted. Any student of history faces the challenge of grasping the many strands that constitute such
world-changing events as wars, social movements, and
environmental disasters. But understanding these significant historic events can be enhanced by exposure
to a variety of perspectives, whether of people involved
intimately or of ones observing from a distance of miles
or years. Understanding can also be increased by learning about the controversies surrounding such events and
exploring hot-button issues from multiple angles. Finally,
true understanding of important historic events involves
knowledge of the events' human impact—of the ways
such events affected people in their everyday lives—all
over the world.

Perspectives on Modern World History examines
global historic events from the twentieth-century onward
by presenting analysis and observation from numerous
vantage points. Each volume offers high school, early
college level, and general interest readers a thematically

arranged anthology of previously published materials that address a major historical event, with an emphasis on international coverage. Each volume opens with background information on the event, then presents the controversies surrounding that event, and concludes with first-person narratives from people who lived through the event or were affected by it. By providing primary sources from the time of the event, as well as relevant commentary surrounding the event, this series can be used to inform debate, help develop critical thinking skills, increase global awareness, and enhance an understanding of international perspectives on history.

Material in each volume is selected from a diverse range of sources, including journals, magazines, newspapers, nonfiction books, personal narratives, speeches, congressional testimony, government documents, pamphlets, organization newsletters, and position papers. Articles taken from these sources are carefully edited and introduced to provide context and background. Each volume of Perspectives on Modern World History includes an array of views on events of global significance. Much of the material comes from international sources and from U.S. sources that provide extensive international coverage.

Each volume in the Perspectives on Modern World History series also includes:

- A full-color **world map**, offering context and geographic perspective.
- An annotated **table of contents** that provides a brief summary of each essay in the volume.
- An **introduction** specific to the volume topic.
- For each viewpoint, a brief **introduction** that has notes about the author and source of the viewpoint, and that provides a summary of its main points.
- Full-color **charts**, **graphs**, **maps**, and other visual representations.

- Informational **sidebars** that explore the lives of key individuals, give background on historical events, or explain scientific or technical concepts.
- A **glossary** that defines key terms, as needed.
- A **chronology** of important dates preceding, during, and immediately following the event.
- A **bibliography** of additional books, periodicals, and Web sites for further research.
- A comprehensive **subject index** that offers access to people, places, and events cited in the text.

Perspectives on Modern World History is designed for a broad spectrum of readers who want to learn more about not only history but also current events, political science, government, international relations, and sociology—students doing research for class assignments or debates, teachers and faculty seeking to supplement course materials, and others wanting to improve their understanding of history. Each volume of Perspectives on Modern World History is designed to illuminate a complicated event, to spark debate, and to show the human perspective behind the world's most significant happenings of recent decades.

INTRODUCTION

For some, the twenty-first century began that horrific day—September 11, 2001—when nineteen terrorists turned four planes into weapons of mass destruction, killing nearly 3,000 people. In the eyes of some observers, such as Indian writer and human rights advocate Shashi Tharoor, the tragic events of that day, now commonly referred to as 9/11, are emblematic of "the relentless forces of globalization."[1] Technological advancements such as cell phones, computers, and planes have eased global communication and the flow of people and money. Indeed, Tharoor claims, "The attackers crossed frontiers easily, coordinated their efforts with technological precision, hijacked planes and crashed them into their targets (as their doomed victims used cell phones to make last-minute calls to loved ones). This was a twenty-first century crime, and it has defined the dangers and the potential of our time as nothing else can."[2] The impact of the events that shocked the world that day makes 9/11 a key date in modern world history.

Nineteen young Arab men began to put their deadly plot into action early on the morning of September 11, when they boarded four airliners departing Boston, Newark, and Washington, DC. Armed only with small knives, box cutters, and cans of Mace, or pepper spray, they took control of the planes shortly after takeoff. Their goal was to destroy what they believed to be symbols of U.S. imperialism, such as the World Trade Center in New York City and the Pentagon in Washington, DC. To destroy these targets, they turned large airliners carrying as much as 10,000 gallons of jet fuel into deadly missiles. At 8:46 A.M., the first airliner flew into the North Tower of the World Trade Center in New York City. At

9:03 A.M., a second airliner struck the South Tower. The burning jet fuel weakened critical support beams in the towers, and less than 90 minutes later, both buildings collapsed. At 9:37 A.M., a third airliner plowed into the Pentagon, and at 10:03 A.M., a fourth, its target believed to be the White House or the U.S. Capitol, crashed into a Pennsylvania field, having been forced down by heroic passengers who knew that the United States was under attack. More than 2,900 people from 90 countries died in the attacks, including the terrorists.

People across the nation—indeed, the world—watched in shock and horror as news outlets broadcast repeatedly the image of United Airlines flight 175 slamming into the South Tower. As firefighters, police, and rescue workers raced to evacuate people from the World Trade Center towers, President George W. Bush was reading to children in a Florida elementary school. After being briefed of the attack and giving a short statement to reporters, Bush was whisked away by the Secret Service to the security of his private jet, Air Force One. Bush was flown around the country until the threat of further attacks diminished. The President then returned to the White House and at 8:30 P.M. addressed the nation, announcing that the United States had been attacked by terrorists. Bush vowed retaliation against the terrorists behind the attack and any nation known to harbor them. He called upon the United States's allies to "stand together to win the war against terrorism."[3] This rhetoric, "either you are with us, or you are with the terrorists,"[4] became part of the Bush doctrine that would shape foreign policy in the years that followed the attacks.

Before Bush returned to the White House that evening, rescue efforts had already begun amid the smoke and ash in New York City and at the Pentagon. Numerous federal agencies were recruited to help. The Federal Emergency Management Agency (FEMA), Environmental Protection

Agency (EPA), and federal law enforcement agencies sent disaster management teams. Although rescue efforts continued for more than a week, the tremendous force of the collapse of the 110-story towers of the World Trade Center, commonly referred to after 9/11 as Ground Zero, left little chance for survivors. Despite a round-the-clock operation that continued throughout the winter, a full excavation and identification of human remains would take more than half a year.

In the days following the attack, patriotism seemed to grip the nation—U.S. flags flew in numbers not seen since World War II, patriotic songs new and old flooded the airwaves, and in unprecedented numbers, people donated money to victims' families and to fire and police associations. Fear nevertheless remained pervasive. Some Americans, ignorant of the distinction between radical Islamic fundamentalism and traditional, nonviolent Muslim religious practices, wrongly assumed that Muslims, or those who appeared to be Muslim, were terrorists. Despite calls by President Bush and other influential leaders to prevent attacks against innocent Arab Americans, amid a rising tide of anger, many Muslims and Arab American communities came under attack. In addition to acts of physical violence, mosques, Hindu temples, and community centers were vandalized and torched. Law enforcement efforts following the attacks also targeted Arab Americans, and hundreds were detained on immigration charges.

To the shock of many Americans, in the streets of some Arab cities, people celebrated the attacks. However, most of the international community responded with an outpouring of sympathy and support. French president Jacques Chirac visited the World Trade Center site, and British prime minister Tony Blair pledged full support in the U.S. war on terrorism. On September 12, the North Atlantic Treaty Organization, an organization of North American and European nations, declared an attack against one member nation to be an attack against all.

On September 14, Congress passed a resolution authorizing the use of military force to fight terrorism, and four weeks later, U.S. and British forces began bombing Afghanistan. On November 13, Kabul, Afghanistan's capital, fell to the allies, ousting the Taliban government that had refused to turn over the terrorist leader, Osama bin Laden, a name with which Americans had become quite familiar.

While 9/11 is remembered foremost for the heartbreaking loss of life, for many Americans the events of that day were a rude awakening to an unfamiliar world. Indeed, most Americans had never heard of Osama bin Laden and his al Qaeda terrorist network, which U.S. officials quickly identified as the unseen hand behind the 9/11 attacks. However, for leaders and policy makers worldwide, that Bin Laden was a potent adversary was made clear in the late 1990s. Bin Laden and his al Qaeda terrorist network were linked to the August 7, 1998, bombing of U.S. embassies in Kenya and Tanzania, which killed 224 people, 12 of whom were Americans. Two weeks later, President Bill Clinton authorized a cruise missile attack against an al Qaeda base in Afghanistan, hoping to kill Bin Laden, who had left the camp before the missile assault.

Americans also struggled to understand why Bin Laden and his followers sought to attack the United States. Explanations for the intense, centuries-old hatred that led to the attacks is subject to rigorous debate, but the modern roots of hatred in the young men who boarded the four planes on 9/11 can be traced to the 1980s. During this time, some young Muslims went to Afghanistan to join the jihad—holy war—against the Soviet Union, which occupied the primarily Muslim nation. Among these was Bin Laden. After the Soviets abandoned the war in Afghanistan, Bin Laden formed al Qaeda to continue jihads against other nations he saw as enemies of the Muslim world. A charismatic leader, Bin Laden appeals to young Muslim men who, according to the 9/11 Commission, are "disoriented by cyclonic change as they confront modernity and globalization."[5] Bin Laden promises to return Islam to its past greatness and restore pride to those who consider themselves victims of foreign oppression. He stresses widely shared grievances in the Muslim world, particularly U.S. foreign policy and the presence of U.S. troops in Saudi Arabia, home to many of Islam's holiest sites, such as Mecca.

The idea to fly airliners into U.S. targets was presented to Bin Laden in late 1998 or early 1999 by Khalid Sheikh Mohammed, one of al Qaeda's field commanders. During 1999, Bin Laden supplied Mohammed with four operatives for the suicide plane attacks, and others were recruited from a cell of extremists who had met in Hamburg, Germany. The tactical commander of the 9/11 terrorist operation—Mohamed Atta—came from this cell. The major planning meeting for 9/11 was held in January 2000 in Kuala Lumpur, Malaysia. Following this meeting, the terrorists responsible for the attack began to enter the United States, where they attended flight schools. Most entered with student or tourist visas, some of which had expired at the time of the attack. How the terrorists could enter the country and prepare themselves for this devastating attack unnoticed was a question to which Americans would later demand an answer.

Shortly following the attacks, public confidence in the efficiency of government agencies was strong, but that confidence would not last. Increased airport security procedures created long lines and delays that most Americans accepted with little complaint. Indeed, nearly every government agency reacted to the attacks with increased security that many believed was necessary, if somewhat inconvenient. With little opposition in the wake of the attacks, Congress passed the USA Patriot

Act, which granted law enforcement broad authority to prevent terrorism, an act that would later prompt a vigorous civil liberties debate. Some claimed, for example, that the definition of terrorism was so broad that it included constitutionally protected speech. Others argued that law enforcement surveillance with little oversight threatened privacy. Indeed, librarians nationwide spoke out against policies that allowed government monitoring of the reading habits of their patrons. In addition, to coordinate efforts to defend the nation against future terrorist attacks, the Bush administration created a new Department of Homeland Security, which in turn led to a major realignment of federal agencies. Whether this restructuring made Americans any safer would also come into question in time.

As time passed and fear and shock abated, however, Americans began to ask questions. It was soon discovered that the Bush administration and U.S. intelligence agencies failed to act on and share vital information that may have prevented the attacks. Under public pressure, in 2002, the Bush administration agreed to an independent investigation of the attacks. The National Commission on Terrorist Attacks Upon the United States, also known as the 9/11 Commission, released its report in July 2004. The commission faulted the administrations of both presidents Clinton and Bush for failing to recognize the danger posed by Osama bin Laden and neglecting to better coordinate counterterrorism agencies. One of the most telling examples was the failure of the CIA and the FBI to follow up on two of the eventual hijackers—Nawaf al Hazmi and Khalid al Mihdhar—who were observed at the Kuala Lumpur meeting in 2000. The CIA tracked both men into the United States, but the FBI claims the CIA never told them. The CIA claims, however, that the information was shared but the FBI failed to act on it. The inquiry also revealed that the FBI failed to act upon suspicions raised by several of its agents, who urged scrutiny of the use of civil aviation schools by those affiliated with terrorist organizations. U.S. intelligence agencies, former agency leaders, and both the Clinton and Bush administrations rebut criticism to this day.

Analysts and experts continue to examine the events of 9/11 with, as the 9/11 Commission aptly notes in its report, "the benefit and handicap of hindsight."[6] The war on terrorism sparked by 9/11 persists as terrorists continue to strike targets in a global jihad. Even now, policy makers worldwide debate laws and policies enacted in the wake of the attacks, and the families of victims, the nation, and the world still mourn. Indeed, people from across the globe visit Ground Zero every day—the scene of what Tharoor terms a twenty-first century crime. How the world responds to terrorism will continue to shape the century. "Our only effective answer to [the terrorists] must be a defiant assertion of our own humanity: to say that each one of us, whoever we are and wherever we are, has the right to live, to love, to hope, to dream, and to aspire to a world in which everyone has that right," Tharoor writes. "That could be the world of the twenty-first century that has just been born," he reflects, "and it could be the most hopeful legacy of the horror that has given it birth."[7]

Notes

1. Shashi Tharoor, "The Global Century," *American Scholar*, Winter 2002.
2. Ibid.
3. George W. Bush, "9/11 Address to the Nation," September 11, 2001.
4. George W. Bush, Address to Joint Session of Congress on the 9/11 Attacks, September 20, 2001.
5. National Commission on Terrorist Attacks Upon the United States, *The 9/11 Commission Report*, July 22, 2004.
6. Ibid.
7. Tharoor, 2002.

World Map

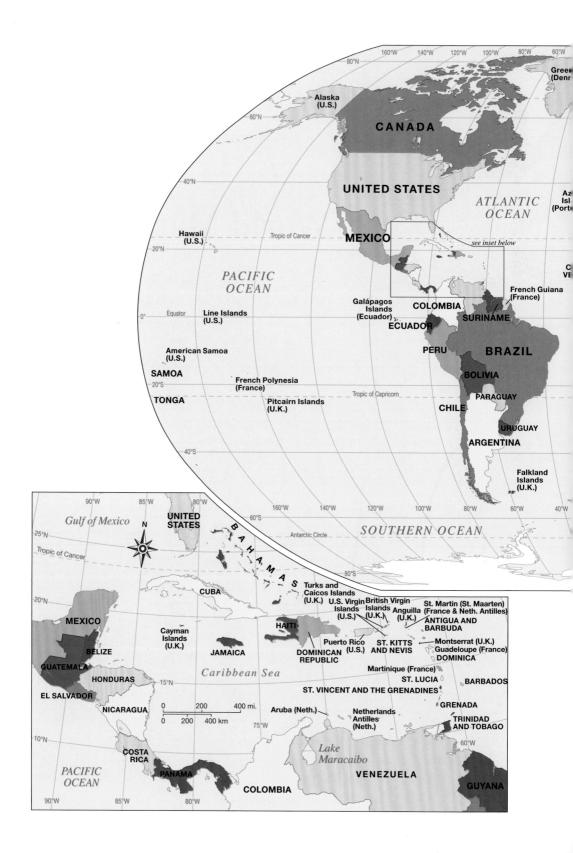

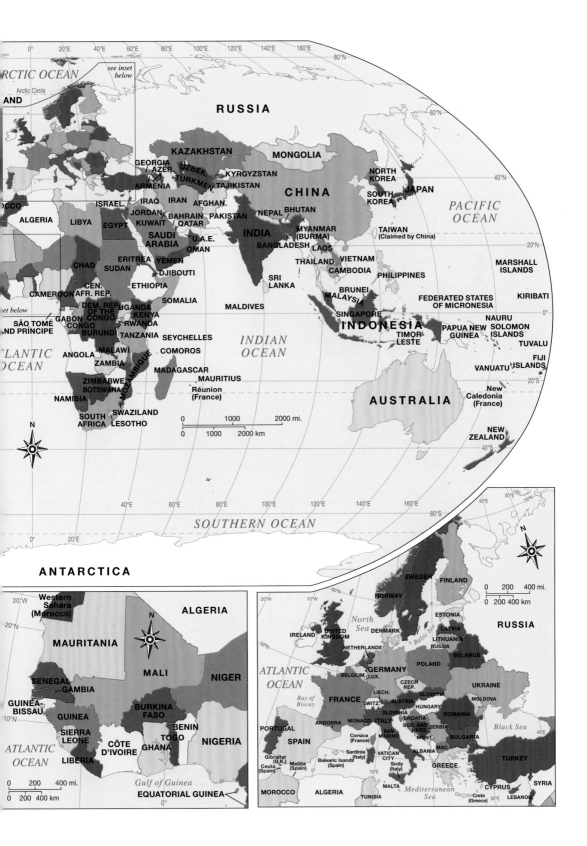

CHAPTER 1

The Events and Aftermath of 9/11

9/11: The Terrorist Attack on the United States

David Greenberg

In the excerpt that follows, David Greenberg, a professor of history and journalism at Rutgers University in New Jersey, summarizes the 9/11 attacks, their impact, and the response. On that fateful morning in 2001, nineteen al Qaeda terrorists hijacked four planes, deliberately crashing two into the World Trade Center in New York City and one into the Pentagon in Washington, DC. The passengers of the fourth overcame the hijackers, and the plane crashed in western Pennsylvania. The attacks halted business and air travel nationwide. However, Greenberg explains, New York City bore the brunt of the attack. Indeed, of the 2,819 people who died that day, most lost their lives in the collapse of the World Trade Center. Congress quickly authorized a military response, Greenberg states. Pervasive

Photo on previous page: News spread quickly the day of the September 11, 2001, attacks, which killed thousands in the United States, destroyed the World Trade Center, and damaged the Pentagon. (Mike Nelson/AFP/Getty Images.)

SOURCE. David Greenberg, *Dictionary of American History, 3rd. Ed.* Belmont, CA: Charles Scribner's Sons, 2003. Copyright © 2003 by Charles Scribner's Sons. Reproduced by permission of Gale, a part of Cengage Learning.

fear also led to dramatic domestic laws and policies that some claim violate civil liberties. Despite worldwide efforts, Greenberg points out, a year later, no end to the war on terrorism seemed in sight.

On Tuesday, 11 September 2001, nineteen members of the Islamic terrorist group Al Qaeda perpetrated a devastating, deadly assault on the United States, crashing airplanes into the Pentagon and the World Trade Center, killing thousands. The attacks shattered Americans' sense of security, threw the nation into a state of emergency, and triggered a months-long war in Afghanistan and an extended worldwide "war on terrorism."

A Devastating Attack

On the morning of 11 September, four teams of terrorists hijacked jetliners departing from Boston; Newark, New Jersey; and Washington, D.C. Once airborne, the terrorists, some of whom had gone to flight school in the United States, murdered the planes' pilots and took control of the aircrafts. At 8:46 A.M., the first plane flew directly into the north tower of the World Trade Center in southern Manhattan, tearing a gaping hole in the building and setting it ablaze. Seventeen minutes later, a second plane flew into the center's south tower, causing similar damage. At 9:43 A.M., a third plane plunged into the Pentagon in Virginia, smashing one wing of the government's military headquarters. The fourth plane appeared headed for Washington, D.C., but at 10:10 A.M. it crashed in western Pennsylvania, apparently after passengers, who had learned of the other attacks through conversations on their cellular phones,[1] rushed the terrorists. Compounding the horror, the south and north towers of the Trade Center, their structures weakened by the heat of the blazes, collapsed entirely, at 10:05 and

10:28 A.M., respectively. The attack was seen as an act of war, likened to Japan's 1941 attack on Pearl Harbor that brought the United States into World War II.

> "Americans responded to the atrocities with shock and panic."

The scope of the carnage and devastation, especially in Manhattan, overwhelmed Americans. Besides the towers, several smaller buildings in the World Trade Center complex also collapsed. People trapped on upper floors of the towers jumped or fell to their deaths. Hundreds of firefighters and rescue crews who had hurried to the buildings were crushed when the towers collapsed. All told, 2,819 people died (because of confusion and difficulty in tracking down individuals, early estimates put the toll at more than 6,000). Thousands more suffered severe physical injury or psychological trauma. Others were displaced from their homes and offices for weeks or months. Some businesses lost large portions of their workforces or sustained financial setbacks. Neighborhood restaurants and shops, which depended on the World Trade Center population for business, struggled to stay solvent.

Shock and Panic

Americans responded to the atrocities with shock and panic. Early in the day, television news reported (but retracted) false rumors of other attacks, including a bombing at the State Department, heightening the uncertainty of what might still happen. States of emergency were declared in Washington and New York. The Federal Aviation Agency grounded all flights in the United States and diverted all incoming foreign air traffic to Canada. Federal officials evacuated the White House and Congress and then closed all federal buildings. The military was put on worldwide alert.

President George W. Bush, attending a political event in Florida, gave a brief statement at 9:30 A.M. noting an "apparent terrorist attack." He then flew around the country, to Air Force bases in Louisiana and Nebraska, as Vice President Dick Cheney supervised operations from a White House bunker. Bush drew criticism for his decision and for promulgating a story, which the White House later admitted was false, that his plane was a target of the terrorists. Shortly before 7 P.M., with the threat of further attacks diminished, Bush returned to the White House. At 8:30 P.M., he spoke from the Oval Office, vowing retaliation against not just the terrorists responsible for the assaults, but also those governments that supported or sheltered them. As Bush's comments suggested, American intelligence agencies already believed the Al Qaeda terrorist ring, run by the Saudi Osama bin Laden, was responsible, and that it was operating in Afghanistan under the protection of the dictatorial Islamic regime known as the Taliban.

As Washington, D.C., coped with a national crisis, New York City faced an unprecedented urban emergency. Businesses closed for the day (and in some cases much longer), as did the subways. Manhattan became a sea of human beings fleeing the lower end of the island by foot. Bridges and tunnels leading into the borough were closed. The municipal primary elections scheduled for that day, including the mayoral contest, were postponed for two weeks. The stock market, located near the Trade Center, closed for the rest of the week. Rudolph Giuliani, the city's controversial mayor, won widespread praise for his confident, candid, and humane public posture during the crisis. In December, *Time* magazine named him "Man of the Year."

> Mostly Egyptians, Saudis, and Yemenis, the perpetrators included both recent immigrants and those who had lived in the United States for several years.

Identifying the Terrorists

American officials had little trouble identifying the terrorists or how they achieved their feat. Mostly Egyptians,

Saudis, and Yemenis, the perpetrators included both recent immigrants and those who had lived in the United States for several years. Some had already been under suspicion but had managed to conceal their whereabouts. Authorities also alleged that Zacarias Moussaoui, a French Muslim of Moroccan descent who had been arrested in August after suspicious behavior at a flight school, was intended to be the twentieth hijacker in the plot.

After the terrorist attacks in New York on September 11, 2001, rescue personnel combed the rubble of the fallen Twin Towers but found few survivors. (**Doug Kanter/AFP/ Getty Images.**)

Officials also determined quickly that the hijackers belonged to bin Laden's Al Qaeda group. For several years, bin Laden had been organizing and bankrolling terrorist activities around the world, directed against the United States, other Western nations and individuals, and pro-Western Arab governments. He worked with a coalition of fanatical Islamic groups, mostly in the Arab world, but also in Southeast and Central Asia, including Egyptians who had assassinated their leader, Anwar Sadat, in 1981. These extremists opposed secular, modern, and Western values, called for the withdrawal of

American troops from Saudi Arabia, and adopted unremitting violence against civilians as their instrument.

Responding to Terrorism

Bin Laden and his associates had struck before. They engineered the 1993 World Trade Center bombing, the 1996 assault on an American military barracks in Saudi Arabia, the 1998 bombings of the American embassies in Kenya and Tanzania, and the 2000 bombing of the USS *Cole*, a destroyer anchored in Yemen. The Bill Clinton administration had responded to these attacks by prosecuting those perpetrators whom it could apprehend, by (unsuccessfully) seeking legal changes to ease the tracking of terrorists, and by launching military strikes in 1998 against Sudan and Afghanistan, which supported Al Qaeda. The administration had also successfully thwarted earlier conspiracies, including a planned series of bombings on New Year's Eve 2000.

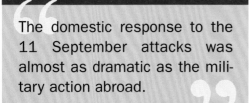

The domestic response to the 11 September attacks was almost as dramatic as the military action abroad.

Few doubted, however, that more-severe reprisals were needed after 11 September. On 14 September, Congress passed a resolution authorizing the use of military force to fight terrorism. The United States also secured a resolution on 12 September from the United Nations Security Council endorsing antiterrorism efforts, which, while not explicitly approving military action, was generally interpreted as doing so. After a mere four weeks—longer than some war hawks wanted—American and British forces began bombing Afghanistan. Despite a massive call-up of military reserves, the U.S. government remained wary of using American ground forces. Instead, Western forces bombed key targets while providing aid and coordination to the Northern Alliance, a coalition of Afghan rebels who did most of the actual fighting. On 13 November, Kabul, Afghanistan's capital, fell to the allies.

On 22 December, a new, interim government friendly to the United States took power.

The Domestic Response

The domestic response to the 11 September attacks was almost as dramatic as the military action abroad. A surge of patriotism gripped the nation. Citizens flew flags, sang "God Bless America," and donated money to the victims' families, the Red Cross, and firefighters' and police officers' associations. The efficient performance of many federal and state agencies—law enforcement, emergency relief, environmental protection, and others—boosted public confidence in government to levels not seen in decades. President Bush appointed Pennsylvania Governor Tom Ridge to his cabinet as the director of "homeland" security, while other officials ordered the closer monitoring of sites ranging from nuclear reactors to reservoirs.

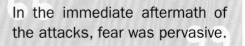

In the immediate aftermath of the attacks, fear was pervasive.

Congress granted new powers to law enforcement officials. The so-called USA Patriot Act, passed in October, gave authorities greater latitude in placing wiretaps and reading E-mail, prompting a national debate about whether civil liberties were being needlessly curtailed. Also controversial was a massive Justice Department dragnet that caught up hundreds of immigrants, mostly Middle Easterners, many of whom were jailed for months for technical violations of immigration laws.

An Atmosphere of Fear

In the immediate aftermath of the attacks, fear was pervasive. For several days, bomb scares proliferated. More troubling, starting in late September, several politicians and prominent news organizations received in the mail packages containing deadly high-grade anthrax spores.

Five people died from the disease, although many more who were exposed recovered by taking antibiotics. Federal officials suspected that the anthrax was circulated not by Al Qaeda terrorists, but by Americans; nonetheless, the weeks-long scare, marked by news of sudden deaths and hospitalizations, fueled Americans' sense of insecurity.

Fear also centered on air travel, which decreased in the short term as many Americans realized how lax airport security was. Airports immediately tightened their security procedures after 11 September, creating long lines and frequent delays, but their policies remained erratic and far from foolproof. Months later, airplanes were still transporting bags that had not been screened, and private firms, not public employees, remained in control. Although air travel rebounded to normal levels, the airlines benefited from a perception after 11 September that they faced bankruptcy, and Congress passed a bailout bill giving them $15 billion in federal subsidies. Republican legislators blocked a plan to extend federal support to laid-off airline employees as well.

Within a few months after the attacks, daily life across America had essentially returned to normal. Fighting in Afghanistan sporadically erupted to top the news, and developments in the "war on terrorism"—whether the apprehension of alleged Al Qaeda members or the administration's plan to create a new cabinet department devoted to domestic security—attracted much comment. But other events, notably a wave of corruption scandals at several leading corporations, also vied for public attention. The war effort, which had successfully ousted the Taliban, still enjoyed wide support, as did President Bush. The administration began planning for an attack on Iraq; although the regime had no demonstrable links to Al Qaeda, its program to develop nuclear and chemical weapons now appeared, in the wake of 11 September, to be an intolerable danger. A year after the 9/11 attack, no end of the "war on terrorism" seemed imminent, as bin Laden and most of his top aides remained at large, and polls showed that a majority of Americans considered it likely that there would be another terrorist attack on their own soil.

Note

1. It was later discovered that few calls were made using individual cell phones. Most were made using the aircraft's built in seatback phones.

The Evolution of the Terrorist Plot

Peter Finn

In the following excerpt, *Washington Post* journalist Peter Finn describes how the 9/11 plot was conceived and developed. In Hamburg, Germany, Finn explains, seven Muslim men were drawn together by a shared commitment to jihad—a holy war against the United States. The men conceived a plan to attack key U.S. targets using commercial aircraft. Fearing accusations of religious persecution due to its Nazi past, the German government was reluctant to target radical Islamic mosques. Thus, Finn states, the Hamburg cell of terrorists met and planned the attacks out in the open. Mohamed Atta, the mastermind of the Hamburg cell, took his plan to al Qaeda leadership, and in Kandahar, Afghanistan, a council of key players met to make final plans. Three members of the Hamburg cell—Atta, Ziad Samir Jarrah, and Marwan Al-Shehhi—died in the attacks.

A round 7 one evening during Ramadan in 1998, the believers filed down a long corridor leading to the prayer room of the Al Muhadjirin mosque [in Hamburg, Germany], placing their shoes on the dark brown shelves before stepping onto a carpet the color of turquoise, a mixture of green for Islam and blue for heaven.

Among the worshipers was a small group of men who clustered around a severe, slight Egyptian named Mohamed Atta. Few words were spoken, but Atta moved with an air of command. Even then he was the "boss," as one of his fellow hijackers, Ziad Samir Jarrah, was to call him in a telephone conversation two days before the Sept. 11 [2001] attacks.

Sheik Adel, a guest speaker from Egypt, read from the Koran, reminded the men of the suffering of their brothers in Palestine and Chechnya, and led a prayer before the daily fast was broken, according to Abderrasak Labied, a 39-year-old Moroccan present that December evening. *"Bismillah,"* the congregation answered, "In the name of Allah."

A large plastic tablecloth was spread on the floor and Atta sat down to eat dates washed down with a glass of milk. Beside him were Ramzi Binalshibh, Said Bahaji and Mounir Motassadeq, three members of what would become known as the Hamburg cell, the core group that carried out the attacks on New York and the Pentagon.

A Commitment to Jihad

These students—a group of seven men that included Marwan Al-Shehhi, Zakariya Essabar and Jarrah—were beginning to coalesce behind a shared commitment to jihad, or holy war. Except for Atta, age 30 at the time, all were in their twenties. Over the next

> Some of the deepest roots of the Sept. 11 attacks were embedded in this windy and prosperous city [Hamburg, Germany] where Islamic extremism was cultivated unnoticed in radical mosques.

year, their common journey would accelerate dramatically under the tutelage of an al Qaeda operative in the city, Mohammed Haydar Zammar, and Atta's increasingly fierce desire to lash out at the United States.

Some of the deepest roots of the Sept. 11 attacks were embedded in this windy and prosperous city where Islamic extremism was cultivated unnoticed in radical mosques, a bookstore with a private backroom stocked with violent texts, informal study groups held at a university meeting place, and roundtable talks in apartments where young men wished death on America.

> Hamburg—and Germany as a whole—was an almost risk-free environment for Islamic radicals.

In one conversation, in November 1999, a German convert to Islam, Shahid Nickels, said to Atta, "Muslims are too weak to do anything against the U.S.A.," according to material collected by German investigators.

"No, something can be done," Atta replied. "There are ways. The U.S.A. is not omnipotent."

Living in Plain Sight

Based on interviews with some of the Hamburg cell's family, friends and associates, some speaking to a reporter for the first time, this account explores the Hamburg milieu that inspired and nurtured the group, and the road the cell followed during the 2½ years of its existence. The story also draws on extensive interviews with U.S. and German intelligence and law enforcement officers as well as on material provided by other European and Arab intelligence agencies about the plot's genesis and trajectory.

The Sept. 11 attacks remain a crime without a complete history. The precise internal mechanics of the plot may never be unlocked. A full exploration of critical elements, such as the recruitment and roles of each of the

15 hijackers from Saudi Arabia, are unknown publicly a year later.

But in Hamburg, key participants in the attacks lived in plain sight. While the Sept. 11 plot evolved in secret, they inhabited a world that was both foreign and familiar to them, providing the strict discipline and focused hatred their plan required to develop, and the freedoms it needed to succeed.

An Ideal Recruiter

The patron of the Hamburg cell was a 300-pound auto mechanic with an inviting manner and war record that made him an ideal recruiter for jihad.

Mohammed Haydar Zammar was born in 1961 in Halab, Syria, and moved to Germany in 1971 with his father. From a religiously conservative family, he impressed acquaintances as exceptionally devout by age 12. He became a regular at Hamburg's mosques, including the Imam Ali mosque, known as the Iranian mosque, and the Al Muhadjirin mosque where many years later Atta would break his Ramadan fast. . . .

In 1991, Zammar decided on a career in jihad, according to an Arab intelligence agency. He traveled to Pakistan on a German passport, then on to an Arab guesthouse in Afghanistan. Zammar underwent training in weapons, explosives and tactics with other Arab fighters. He was then assigned to a second, elite camp near Jalalabad.

Although al Qaeda's leader, Osama bin Laden, was living in Sudan at the time, the organization had established training camps in the eastern part of Afghanistan under the protection of the warlord Gulbuddin Hekmatyar. Zammar fought alongside Hekmatyar's troops against the communist Afghan regime. . . .

Hamburg—and Germany as a whole—was an almost risk-free environment for Islamic radicals. German officials, mindful of the country's Nazi past, say now that they were reluctant to target mosques and risk allegations of racism or religious persecution. Such reservations meant that while authorities were aware of the calls to arms that fired up the members of the Hamburg cell, they saw no cause to intervene.

As a full-fledged apostle of jihad, Zammar quickly became one of the best known figures in the tight, extremist Islamic community in Hamburg. He railed against the United States and the West.

"We cannot just sit and do nothing," Zammar said in a speech about the West's injustices against Islam, according to Azam Irschid, deputy director of the Al Muhadjirin mosque. "Who are the worst terrorists?" Zammar shouted on another occasion. "The so-called civilized world." . . .

Among those at the table with Zammar were young men from Somalia, Ethiopia, Algeria and Morocco, whom Zammar regaled with stories from the front lines of the holy war, Labied recalled.

The big man was looking for volunteers.

Connections at the Mosque

Mohamed Atta got to know Zammar in the Al Quds mosque in Hamburg, most likely in 1998, according to U.S., German and Arab sources. Atta had arrived in Hamburg in 1992 and later enrolled at the Technical University of Hamburg-Harburg. A disciplined student and pious Muslim, Atta was reserved and aloof, particularly in the company of Germans.

Among fellow Muslims, he could be a hectoring moralist. He chastised Ziad Samir Jarrah and Marwan Al-Shehhi for their affection for music, alcohol and cigarettes until his two young companions also renounced the trappings of Western indulgence. . . .

By 1998, when he met Zammar, Atta had been a regular at the mosque for at least four years. He also had attended study groups run by a local radical, Mohammed bin Nasser Belfas. Atta visited the Attawhid bookstore where literature and videos on jihad were sold from a backroom that the public could not enter.

These places were the first of several local hubs for the Hamburg cell. Its members had come to Germany as students from different Arab countries between 1992 and 1997. After attending a variety of colleges, they met in Hamburg between the mid- and late 1990s, according to Kay Nehm, Germany's lead federal prosecutor.

The Cell Forms

Mounir Motassadeq, for instance, met Atta in 1995 and the following year was a signatory to Atta's will. Motassadeq later introduced Atta to both Said Bahaji, a German Moroccan, and Zakariya Essabar, a Moroccan. Atta met Al-Shehhi, from the United Arab Emirates, at a German language school in Bonn in 1997. Jarrah, from Lebanon, came into the circle through Essabar. Ramzi Binalshibh, an asylum-seeker from Yemen, met the group through the Al Quds mosque.

> By the fall of 1999, members of the Hamburg cell had agreed among themselves to plan a spectacular attack using commercial aircraft.

Others floated into the circle, but for one reason or another were cast aside. Through friendship, belief and ambition, these seven crystallized as a unit: Atta, Al-Shehhi, Jarrah, Binalshibh, Bahaji, Motassadeq and Essabar.

"The mastermind of the group was . . . Atta," Nehm said. "He was considered the boss of the group on grounds of his age, his longer stay in Germany and the resulting good language skills, but also on grounds of his organizing talents and his persuasiveness."

In November 1998, Atta, Binalshibh and Bahaji moved into an apartment on Marien Street near the university. Al-Shehhi also lived there occasionally, and

Motassadeq, Essabar and Jarrah met the others for long discussions in the apartment.

Zammar was a frequent visitor, but quickly he was eclipsed by Atta as the voice of authority. Zammar was respected mostly for his contacts with an international network. . . .

Plans to Use Aircraft

By the fall of 1999, members of the Hamburg cell had agreed among themselves to plan a spectacular attack using commercial aircraft, according to German investigators. This view challenges some assumptions that the Sept. 11 plot was devised entirely by the al Qaeda leadership and imparted on the hijackers during their training in Afghanistan.

"At the latest in October 1999, [the Hamburg's group radicalization] led to the idea of attacking the United States using airplanes, a concept possibly inspired by ideas from other representatives of the international network," Nehm said. "The group members then traveled to Afghanistan in order to discuss details with members of the international network and to obtain financial and logistical support."

Supporting this thesis, according to a summary of the German investigation, are witness statements and the discovery by German police of a file on flight simulators on the computer of one of the Hamburg conspirators. The material was downloaded in 1999. There is no evidence, according to the German investigation, that anyone in the Hamburg cell traveled to Afghanistan before November 1999. . . .

In an interview scheduled for broadcast this week [in September 2002] by the al-Jazeera network, [Khalid Sheik] Mohammed [believed to be the logistical mastermind of the 9/11 attacks] said "about 2½ years prior to the holy raids on Washington and New York, the military committee held a meeting during which we decided

Photo on previous page: Two Old Town buildings—The town hall and St. Nicholas Church—tower over Hamburg, Germany where the 9/11 plot unfolded. (DEA/C. Sappa/De Agostini/Getty Images.)

to start planning for a martyrdom operation inside America."

An article in the *Sunday Times* of London by the al-Jazeera journalist who conducted the interview, Yosri Fouda, cites Mohammed and Binalshibh taking credit for the Sept. 11 attacks. Mohammed said it was his idea to target prominent buildings in the United States, and he said Atta and other operatives were earmarked as pilots sometime in 1999. He said al Qaeda had first considered hitting nuclear installations.

Others in the al Qaeda leadership shared a vision of an airborne attack. According to the interrogation of al Qaeda suspects in Jordan, Muhammad Atef, bin Laden's Egyptian military operations chief, had seized on the idea in late 1999 after American investigators said an Egypt Airlines pilot had committed suicide by crash-diving his plane into the Atlantic Ocean in October 1999.

Against this background, when Atta slipped into Afghanistan from Pakistan in late 1999 in the company of al Qaeda escorts, he was carrying an idea that would resonate with his handlers.

Training and Meetings

The first to leave Hamburg for Afghanistan was Jarrah on Nov. 25, 1999. He flew to Karachi, Pakistan, via Istanbul on Turkish Airlines. Four days later, Atta followed, taking the same route. Al-Shehhi and then Binalshibh went next, although German investigators have not uncovered exact routes for the last two. Bahaji, Essabar and Motassadeq would not follow until spring 2000, according to German officials.

In Afghanistan, the new arrivals were taken to a guesthouse in Kandahar, called the Al-Ghumad House after the Saudi Al-Ghamdi

> Drawn from al Qaeda's Department of Martyrs, [thirteen men] would become known by U.S. investigators as 'the muscle,' whose mission was to subdue the passengers and crew of the aircraft.

tribe, according to the al-Jazeera interviews. There they met three Saudis in what Binalshibh described to al-Jazeera as a *shura*, or council, of the future pilots and key players.

Waiting in Kandahar was Khalid Almihdhar, a former Red Sea fisherman who came from Mecca, and Nawaf Alhazmi, a merchant also from Mecca, according to interviews with officials at the Saudi Interior Ministry's offices in Jiddah.

Both of them would die on American Airlines Flight 77, which struck the Pentagon. Also present in Kandahar, the Arab network reported, was the pilot of that flight, Hani Hanjour, from Naif, southeast of Jiddah. A former resident of the United States, he was frustrated in his desire to become a pilot for Saudi Airlines.

Around these three Saudis and the Hamburg group, the plot would be constructed by al Qaeda. Al Qaeda would make up the rest of the teams of hijackers with 12 recruits drawn from Saudi tribes that bin Laden was familiar with and another hijacker from the United Arab Emirates, Fayez Rashid Ahmed Hassan Al Qadi Banihammad, also known as Fayez Ahmed.

Mohammed claimed these 13 men were drawn from al Qaeda's Department of Martyrs. They would become known by U.S. investigators as "the muscle," whose mission was to subdue the passengers and crew of the aircraft while the planes were commandeered by the plot's leaders.

In January 2000, as Atta underwent training in Afghanistan, a further meeting occurred that tied the Hamburg cell to the rest of the hijackers. Binalshibh, Almihdhar and Alhazmi met in Kuala Lumpur, Malaysia, in the presence of another al Qaeda operative, Tawfiq bin Atash, a one-legged veteran of Afghanistan.

Binalshibh, a Yemeni, is a relative of Almihdhar's wife. Almihdhar came from a prominent Yemeni family with longtime links to al Qaeda, and obtained Saudi citi-

North Sea

Baltic Sea

SWEDEN

DENMARK

NETHERLANDS

Hamburg

POLAND

★ Berlin

GERMANY

BELGIUM

CZECH REPUBLIC

LUXEMBOURG

FRANCE

AUSTRIA

0   150

Miles

SWITZERLAND

ITALY

Taken from: *Washington Post*, www.washingtonpost.com

zenship in 1996, according to Interior Ministry officials in Jiddah.

The January meeting was photographed by Malaysian intelligence and al Qaeda is believed to have discussed an attack on the USS *Cole* in Yemen, which occurred later that year, as well as a strike on American soil.

By now the plot was accelerating.

The Plot Moves Forward

Immediately after the Malaysian gathering, Almihdhar and Alhazmi flew to Los Angeles and quickly enrolled in a flight school north of San Diego.

In late February 2000, Atta and the other Hamburg pilots began to return to Germany from Afghanistan. They declared their passports stolen to cover incriminating stamps and began to contact flight schools in the United States to obtain visas to enter the country.

The members of the cell already knew they would attack New York, according to German officials, citing a statement by Al-Shehhi. In April or May, Al-Shehhi mentioned the World Trade Center as a target in a conversation in Hamburg with a female librarian, said Nehm, the prosecutor.

"There will be thousands of dead," Al-Shehhi told the librarian, according to Nehm. "You will all think of me."

The librarian later came forward as a witness, according to the federal prosecutor's office, which declined to identify her or say when she provided the information.

In the interview with al-Jazeera, Binalshibh said that Al-Shehhi, even before he learned of the operation, "used to have beautiful visions that he flies in the sky with huge green birds and crashes into things."

"What things?" asked the al-Jazeera interviewer.

"Just things," Binalshibh said.

Binalshibh also wished to participate in the attacks, as did Essabar, but both had their U.S. visa applications rejected. The indictment of Zacarias Moussaoui, a 34-year-old French national, alleges that Moussaoui was picked to replace Binalshibh in December 2000. That month, Binalshibh flew to London to meet Moussaoui, who then left Britain for Pakistan.

Scouting the Targets

Binalshibh told al-Jazeera that the pilots scouted their targets and assigned them code names: The twin towers were called the Faculty of Town Planning, an apparent coy reference to Atta's studies, in which he railed against skyscrapers. The Pentagon was the Faculty of Fine Arts. And the Capitol, which Binalshibh told al-Jazeera was the target of the plane that crashed in Pennsylvania, was the Faculty of Law.

> " Only three members of the Hamburg cell—Atta, Jarrah and Al-Shehhi—died on Sept. 11. "

Money for the pilots was routed by an al Qaeda operative in Dubai named Moustaffa Ahmed al-Hazemi, according to U.S. investigators. On March 1, Essabar and Binalshibh moved out of the apartment on Marien Street, leaving it cleaned. . . .

The Muscle

Over the summer, the 13 hijackers known as "the muscle" began to arrive in the United States. Bin Laden himself appears to have had a role in directly choosing these hijackers, and he clearly wanted Saudis. "They were selected for their fervor, their discipline and their nationality," said one Arab official. . . .

The Saudi government, without providing any hard evidence, asserts that the Saudi "muscle" was recruited outside Saudi Arabia after these men had left to fight in Chechnya. The Saudi interior minister, Prince Nayef, said in an interview that he also believes most of these late volunteers did not know they were going to die on Sept. 11.

But the government offered little support for its theses. In interviews at the Interior Ministry in Jiddah, Saudi officials said their files on the 15 Saudi hijackers consisted only of basic biographical material such as date of birth, employment and marital status, date of passport issue and when they left the kingdom.

An alleged al Qaeda video released to al-Jazeera and broadcast Tuesday [September 10, 2002] suggests, however, that the Saudi volunteers knew exactly what they were doing. . . .

By August 2001, his disciples departed, bin Laden began to speak to followers of a dream he had, according to [Zuher Hilal Mohamed al] Tbaiti, [an alleged terrorist held] prisoner in Morocco. "He said he saw America in ashes," Tbaiti told his interrogators. "It was like a prophecy."

Only three members of the Hamburg cell—Atta, Jarrah and Al-Shehhi—died on Sept. 11. Essabar, Bahaji and Binalshibh fled Germany shortly before the attacks; all three are being sought on an international arrest warrant issued by German officials. Motassadeq was indicted in Germany last month on at least 3,116 counts of accessory to murder.

As for Zammar, the recruiter, he was arrested in Morocco last year and deported to Syria, where he is being interrogated.

New York: A Changed City

Jim Dwyer and Susan Sachs

New York City changed on 9/11, claim journalists Jim Dwyer and Susan Sachs in the following *New York Times* article published the day after the attacks. Normally assertive and sometimes impatient New Yorkers were stunned into silence and eas- ily moved to tears and tenderness. Masses of Manhattan's shocked refugees trudged on foot to escape the destruction. Along the way, they asked themselves and others how some- thing like this could happen. Parents wondered how they would explain the disaster to their children. As their fellow New Yorkers marched out of Manhattan, the authors explain, people shared water, dust masks, and news. Some sought out places of wor- ship that provided food, coffee, and solace. Dwyer and Sachs assert that everyone in New York was touched in some way by the attack on the World Trade Center that tragic day.

SOURCE. Jim Dwyer and Susan Sachs, "A Tough City Is Swept by Anger, Despair and Helplessness," *New York Times*, September 12, 2001, p. A6. Copyright © 2001 by The New York Times Company. Reproduced by permission.

The city changed yesterday. No one, no matter how far from Lower Manhattan, could step on a New York sidewalk untouched by concussions.

The day began in the brilliance of a late summer morning, then was obscured in gray balls of dust and smoke that seemed to touch everyone. The city had become an empire of the stricken.

Erin Dubin, 26 and an aspiring Broadway dancer from Minnesota, had started the day with an audition for *Footloose*, hoping for her big break. At midmorning, tears rolling down her face and a cell phone dangling from her limp hand, she stood stock still on 43rd Street at Seventh Avenue, staring but barely taking in the news ticker across the street. Her boyfriend worked at Lehman Brothers in the World Trade Center as a Web page designer.

Normally he arrived at work at 9 A.M. and Ms. Dubin fervently hoped he had been delayed. But she could not reach him.

"I hope he was late," she said, frozen in place as the words scrolled endlessly across the buildings at Times Square. "I don't know exactly what I should be doing. Where should I go?"

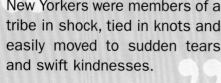

New Yorkers were members of a tribe in shock, tied in knots and easily moved to sudden tears and swift kindnesses.

A Tribe in Shock

New Yorkers were members of a tribe in shock, tied in knots and easily moved to sudden tears and swift kindnesses. People moved through Midtown without the ordinary get-out-of-my-way pace. They listened to radios. They grabbed one-minute updates from strangers. They spoke urgently into cell phones. They waited quietly in long lines—no shoving, no impatient words—at the pay phones on street corners. The hundreds who sat or stood under outdoor jumbo electronic television screens were virtually silent; it was no time for small talk.

Further uptown on Eighth Avenue, a crowd stood around a delivery van, listening to radio reports.

By midmorning, when the news had filtered out to just about everybody and the great cloud of black smoke at the southern end of Manhattan had become a permanent blot on the horizon, businesses began to close down and bars began to fill up. Smokers who had quit decided to take it up again, at least for the day. A bus would stop, going uptown, and people rushed to get on, no matter what its destination.

"Will someone ask the driver where this bus is going?" shouted a woman as she propelled herself toward an M2 limited bus on Madison Avenue. "Just get on or you'll never get out of Manhattan," called back a teenager near the front.

But getting places was out of the question for most people. The only way to go was north, or east, away from the fires and destruction. And for most, the only way to go was on foot. They found bridges closed and highways open to pedestrians and subways stopped dead.

Jim Speziale, driving a bread delivery truck, took pity. He stopped his truck on Park Avenue at 33rd Street, opened the door and invited

> There were refugees everywhere: a long, slow motion flight from the core of the city, great strings of people putting their feet on the ground, in hopes that it, unlike the sky, was safe.

people in. "I'm going up as far as 59th Street," he shouted to the crowds on the sidewalks. They climbed in by the dozens.

People who made it across the Manhattan Bridge were met by workers from Long Island College Hospital and Brooklyn Hospital Center. They were handing out water and fruit juice to those beginning to trudge down Flatbush Avenue.

"Water and medical attention here!" shouted Claudine Rose, normally a clerical worker at the Brooklyn Hospital

Center. "You can call your families across the street and let people know that you're okay."

It was almost as if the city had turned tender, as if people wanted to tip-toe around each other so as not to cause any upset. Normal reactions—irritation at stalled traffic, peevishness at pedestrians who stopped in the middle of the sidewalk—were muted.

> How could this horror, which would not be credible on a movie screen, be actual, be real, be flesh and blood?

A Slow Motion Flight

There were refugees everywhere: a long, slow motion flight from the core of the city, great strings of people putting their feet on the ground, in hopes that it, unlike the sky, was safe. And because they would be putting down their feet many times, some women stopped on Canal Street to buy $8 flip-flops, a small advantage over high-heeled shoes for such a journey.

As those brushed by the attacks drifted away from the neighborhood around ground zero, they were met with acts of grace, large and small. Keith Vance reported that he found himself a few blocks away from the collapse, in front of a Chinese delicatessen. The proprietor came out with bottles of water. Then a man in a hardware store handed out dust masks used by plasterers.

The numbers of walkers grew as the devastating news took hold. Maria Thomas, at work in Macy's when she heard about the explosions, decided not to stay. "Look, Macy's is a landmark building, you know," she explained from 10 blocks away. As she left, customers were streaming into the store, apparently unaware of what was happening in Lower Manhattan. "It's believable and at the same time it's not believable," said Ms. Thomas.

That was the mental line many people walked: how could this horror, which would not be credible on a movie screen, be actual, be real, be flesh and blood?

For some of those who had been downtown, the horror of the moment emerged as they walked miles toward home, carried along on waves of shock and contemplation. Ed Lamm, who works at J.P. Morgan in New York Plaza, said he could not escape the image.

"It's devastating, just looking back at that scene," said Mr. Lamm, 53, of Mineola, as he crossed the Manhattan Bridge. "The smoke, the darkness. It's like the day stood still.

"You're aware what's in the sky, checking for planes, seeing F-15's in the sky. But we're the lucky ones, we're alive."

What Happens Next?

Carole Kitrosser, a financial planner who normally works a few blocks from the World Trade Center, was seeing clients uptown yesterday. Her country would never feel the same. "If they can stop New York City from functioning, what happens next?" Ms. Kitrosser said. She said she felt "violated."

"I don't think I can ever go downtown to work again," Ms. Kitrosser said. "I don't think I can look at the rubble. Our schools are closed. Our financial district is closed. We're not safe anywhere."

For those at a distance, the pace of events—one crash, a second crash, a collapse and then another—brought a slow-motion fear, rising like a tide into consciousness. In Brooklyn Heights, Lisa Morris heard a radio report about the first plane crashing into the tower, and walked onto the street to look across the harbor.

"The first building was in flames and the second plane came right across and went into the second building," she said. "It must have flown over the Statue of Liberty and come right in.

"It was strange to think that the first crash was a horrible accident. And the second, knowing it wasn't an accident, made it so much worse," Ms. Morris said.

> As hard to absorb as adults found the day's events, their worries for children were of another order of magnitude.

Moved by the television and radio coverage, lines of volunteers turned up at hospitals across the city, prepared to donate blood for the survivors. Many were turned away because the hospitals were not ready to accept them, or actually found themselves with enough on hand—and too few survivors in need of it.

In the Gristede's at Broadway and 108th Street, David McCarthy, 40, was one of many buying jugs of water, "just in case." He added: "I went to the bank, and all the banks except one were closed. And I realized, wait a minute, something's going to happen."

Anxious Parents

As hard to absorb as adults found the day's events, their worries for children were of another order of magnitude.

"What am I going to tell my daughter?" said Carmen Diaz, who was sent home from her Midtown office along with other employees and was wandering around, hugging a transistor radio, until her daughter's school let out at 3 P.M. "I don't even know myself why such a thing could happen. It will be so hard to explain."

Within an hour of the disaster, hundreds of anxious parents had massed at Public School 192, a school that serves many Dominican immigrants in West Harlem. Some feared a world war would break out, and wanted to protect their children. Others said that if the World Trade Center had been destroyed, then why shouldn't a school be next? Most said that when they heard the news they simply wanted their children to be with them. By 11:40 A.M., parents had picked up all but 150 of the 1,700 students in the school.

Elton Callender, who came to get his nephew, a first grader, said he did not want the boy to hear the news from a stranger and panic. "I just need to explain this stuff to him," Mr. Callender said. "Actually, I'm scared that there could be a world war."

As another boy and his father walked home, tightly holding hands, the boy said: "Papi, did you notice that some people blew up a house?" His father corrected him. "Blew up the World Trade Center."

> Many sought solace in prayers, either alone or in the great holy spaces of the city.

"Wha?" the boy exclaimed. "I thought it was a house. And some people died, right?"

"Right," his father said tersely, and kept walking.

Seeking Solace

Many sought solace in prayers, either alone or in the great holy spaces of the city. Tom Brown, a street corner preacher on Broadway and Canal, had handed out about 500 tracts in 90 minutes. "People think this stuff is baloney, but today they're listening," Mr. Brown said.

At 9 A.M. a bell at the Cathedral Church of St. John the Divine began tolling in the slow, steady rhythm of mourning. In the evening, Cardinal Edward M. Egan said Mass at St. Patrick's Cathedral, praising the efforts of rescue workers and those providing medical care. "I saw New York at its best," he said. "I saw police officers and firefighters careless of their own safety, interested in only serving this great city, covered in soot. I saw many of them bleeding from the necks and arms. They're New York at its best. They inspired this New Yorker with pride."

The cardinal said that he had administered last rites to 12 to 15 of the injured who were taken to St. Vincent's Manhattan Hospital. He said one of them died about six minutes later. At one point while he was at St. Vincent's, he looked up and saw the second tower collapse. "It was a nightmare, a nightmare for this city of noble and decent people."

Places of worship all over the city propped open their doors, offering everything from pasta and coffee to a spiritual perspective. And what might normally be seen as unwelcome proselytizing was embraced. At the Middle Collegiate Church on Second Avenue in the East Village, a congregant stood on the steps, urging anyone who paused to come on in. Many took him up on it: people covered in soot, a man who had watched his co-worker die, a woman who worked on the 19th floor of one of the towers and could not reach her daughter.

"There's nothing but death in the air today," said Debbi Gibson, a paralegal who lives in East Harlem. "I don't want to hate anybody. I don't want to judge anybody. So in order to keep my peace I had to be here for a little bit."

Even those who offered solace were not untouched by the tragedy. In the basement of St. Joseph's Church in Greenwich Village, Veronica Johnson, a parishioner, busied herself over a counter laden with food meant for rescue workers, pulling her sunglasses on as she struggled with news that the body of a familiar friend, the Rev. Michael Judge, had been identified. Father Judge was a Fire Department chaplain. "He married my son. He baptized the kids. He's been there for everybody," she said, her face suddenly damp.

Photo on previous page: New Yorkers, little known for public sentimentality, found themselves moved to acts of tenderness in the aftermath of the attacks. (Dave Hogan/ Getty Images.)

A French Journalist Claims That We Are All Americans

Jean-Marie Colombani

The day after the 9/11 attacks, Jean-Marie Colombani, editor of the French newspaper, *Le Monde*, wrote the following article, "Nous Sommes Tous Américains" [We Are All Americans]. Colombani claims that the French feel a strong solidarity with Americans. However, he fears that the United States, as the sole superpower, has no counterbalance now that the Cold War is over. Now that the United States no longer offers itself as a better model than the Soviets, Colombani asserts, it draws only hate. Thus, rather than establish Islamic fundamentalism as the new enemy, he urges the United States to avoid the anti-Islamic reflex and choose policies that draw nations to it rather than encourage others to follow in the footsteps of terrorists. Colombani now heads the French version of *Slate*, an online editorial newsmagazine.

SOURCE. Jean-Marie Colombani, "We Are All Americans," *Le Monde Daily*, September 12, 2001, English version. Copyright © Le Monde.fr. Reproduced by permission.

In this tragic moment, when words seem so inadequate to express the shock people feel, the first thing that comes to mind is this: We are all Americans! We are all New Yorkers, just as surely as John F. Kennedy declared himself to be a Berliner in 1962 when he visited Berlin. Indeed, just as in the gravest moments of our own history, how can we not feel profound solidarity with those people, that country, the United States, to whom we are so close and to whom we owe our freedom, and therefore our solidarity? How can we not be struck at the same time by this observation: The new century has come a long way.

A New Age

Sept. 11, 2001, marks the ushering in of a new age that seems so far from the promise of another historic day, Nov. 9, 1989 [the fall of the Berlin Wall], and a somewhat euphoric year, 2000, which we thought might conclude with peace in the Middle East.

And so a new century moves ahead, with powerful technology, as shown by the sophistication of the war operation that struck America's symbols: those of its enormous economic power in the heart of Manhattan [and] of its military might at the Pentagon. The beginnings of this century defy understanding unless you promptly and indiscriminately subscribe to the cliché that is already the most widespread: the triggering of a war of the South against the North.[1]

But to say this would be to credit the perpetrators of this murderous madness with "good intentions," or with some plan, whereby the oppressed peoples would be avenged against their sole oppressor, America. That would have allowed them to claim "poverty" as their authority, thus committing an affront to it! What mon-

> America, in the solitude of its power, in its status as the sole superpower . . . seems to draw nothing but hate.

strous hypocrisy! None of those who had a hand in this operation can claim they intend the good of humanity. Actually, they have no interest in a better world. They simply want to wipe ours off the face of the Earth.

A World with No Counterbalance

The reality is more certainly that of a world with no counterbalance, physically destabilized, and thus more dangerous since there is no multipolar balance. And

A flag burning in Egypt illustrates the anger and hatred toward the United States that is fanned by al Qaeda and others. (**AFP/Getty Images.**)

America, in the solitude of its power, in its status as the sole superpower, now in the absence of a Soviet counter-model, has ceased to draw other nations to itself; or more precisely, in certain parts of the globe, it seems to draw nothing but hate. In the regulated world of the Cold War, where the various kinds of terrorism were more or less aided by Moscow, a certain degree of control was still possible, and the dialogue between Moscow and Washington never stopped. In today's monopolistic world, it is a new barbarism, apparently with no control, which seems to want to set itself up as a counter-power. Perhaps, even in Europe, from the Gulf War to the use of F-16s by the Israeli army against the Palestinians, we have underestimated the intensity of the hate, which, from the outskirts of Jakarta to those of Durban, among the rejoicing crowds in Nablus and Cairo, is focused against the United States.

> In the eyes of American public opinion and its leadership, Islamic fundamentalism, in all its forms, risks being designated as the new enemy.

But the reality is perhaps also that of an America whose own cynicism has caught up with [it]. If Bin Laden, as the American authorities seem to think, really is the one who ordered the Sept. 11 attacks, how can we fail to recall that he was in fact trained by the CIA and that he was an element of a policy, directed against the Soviets, that the Americans considered to be wise? Might it not then have been America itself that created this demon?

A New Course for America

Be that as it may, America is going to change. Profoundly. America is like a large ocean liner, sailing for a long time on the same course. When the course is changed, it is changed for a long time. And, even though the expression may be overworked, the United States has suffered an unprecedented shock. Pearl Harbor marked the end of isolationism, so deeply rooted that it was not even moved by Hitler's barbarity. After Pearl Harbor, everything changed. And America accepted it all, from the Marshall Plan to sending GIs to every point of the globe. Then came the Vietnam debacle, which led to a new doctrine, that of the rare but massive use of force, accompanied by the dogma of "zero casualties" for the United States, as illustrated during the Gulf War. All of that has now been swept away. There is no doubt that every means will be employed against enemies who, up to now, have remained elusive.

The new hand that has begun to be dealt out in blood, at this stage, will bring with it at least two foreseeable consequences. Both have to do with alliances: It is certainly the end of an entire strategy conceived in opposition to Russia, the Soviet Union at the time. Russia, at least in its non-Islamic areas, is going to become the main ally of the United States. Perhaps it is also the end of an alliance that the United States had traced out in the 1930s and soundly established in the 1950s with Sunni Muslim fundamentalism, such as it is defended particularly in Saudi Arabia and Pakistan. In the eyes of American public opinion and its leadership, Islamic fundamentalism, in all its forms, risks being designated as the new enemy. Indeed, the anti-Islamic reflex, immediately after the attack on a federal building in Oklahoma City, resulted in statements that were ridiculous, if not downright odious.

A Barbarous Logic

Beyond their obvious murderous madness, these latest attacks nonetheless follow a certain logic.

Obviously it is a barbarous logic, marked by a new nihilism that is repugnant to the great majority of those who believe in Islam, which, as a religion, does not condone suicide any more than Christianity does, and certainly not suicide coupled with the massacre of innocent people. But it is a political logic, which, by going to extremes, seeks to force Muslim opinion to "choose sides" against those who are currently designated as "the Great Satan." By doing this, their objective might well be to spread and deepen an unprecedented crisis in the Arab world.

In the long term, this attitude is obviously suicidal, because it attracts lightning. And it might attract a bolt of lightning that does not discriminate. This situation requires our leaders to rise to the occasion. They must act so that the peoples whom these warmongers are seeking to win over and are counting on will not fall in step behind them in their suicidal logic. This we can say with some dread: Modern technology allows them to go even further. Madness, even under the pretext of despair, is never a force that can regenerate the world. That is why today we are all Americans.

> Madness, even under the pretext of despair, is never a force that can regenerate the world. That is why today we are all Americans.

Note

1. The author refers to a socioeconomic and political division between the wealthy developed countries, which generally occupy the northern hemisphere, and the poorer, less developed countries, which generally occupy the southern hemisphere.

A Muslim Leader Calls for Restraint

El Hassan bin Talal

In the following article, published the day after the 9/11 attacks, Jordanian prince El Hassan bin Talal expresses his outrage at the attacks on the United States. However, he urges restraint. Middle East nations know well that violence begets violence. He therefore asks that the international community not overreact and instead develop a consensus on how best to fight terrorism. In addition, Prince Talal explains that all religions reject terrorism and asks that in response to this horrible crime, people not single out Muslim communities. Prince Talal is the grandson of King Talal, who brought democratic reforms to Jordan, considered one of the most progressive nations in the Arab world. In September 2001, Prince Talal was appointed Special Advisor to the current King of Jordan, Abdullah II.

SOURCE. El Hassan bin Talal, "A Muslim Calls for Sanity," *Jordan Times*, September 12, 2001. Copyright © 2001 Jordan Times. Reproduced by permission.

Not as Moderator of the World Conference on Religion and Peace, nor as a Muslim directly descended from the Prophet Mohammad, but as a member of our common human family, I wish to express my deepest condolences to the families, friends and colleagues who have lost loved ones in the heinous attacks in New York and other cities of the United States of America Sept. 11, 2001. I further extend my deepest sympathy to the people of the United States of America, to all concerned humanity and to President George W. Bush.

The world's faithful stand aghast at the tragedy that has befallen ordinary people of all nations and faiths who live within the United States, and I condemn unequivocally this outrage against humanity.

Respecting the sanctity of life is the cornerstone of all great faiths. Such acts of extreme violence, in which innocent men, women and children are both the targets and the pawns, are totally unjustifiable. No religious tra-

BACKLASH: POST–SEPTEMBER 11 VIOLENCE AGAINST ARAB AND MUSLIM AMERICANS

Type of Incident	Number
Airport Profiling	191
Bomb Threats	16
Deaths	11
Death Threats	56
Discrimination at Schools	74
Discrimination at Work	166
Hate Mail	315
Intimidation by Law Enforcement	224
Physical Assault/Property Damage	289
Public Harassment	372
Total Incidents	**1,717**

Taken from: Timothy G. Borden, "September 11, 2001: The United States is Attacked on its Own Soil," History Behind the Headlines: The Origins of Conflicts Worldwide, Vol. 5, eds. Sonia G. Benson et al. Farmington Hills, MI: Gale, 2002.

> In the aftermath of this heinous crime, there is the risk that specific communities, such as the Muslims, will face violent repercussions.

dition can or will tolerate such behaviour and all will loudly condemn it.

Terrorism is by nature indiscriminate, killing civilians of all ages, colours and persuasions; it intimidates individuals and communities the world over; its very existence depends upon its ability to perpetuate fear; it is perhaps the most dreadful tool used to express violence.

The proliferation of terrorist cells operating throughout the world challenges us all, particularly governments, which will have to address this provocation at all levels in the 21st century. A piecemeal approach will not do. Nor will a reaction based upon conjecture as to whom might be responsible. In times like these, it is easy to act immediately and to think things through only once irrevocable decisions have been made.

A Call for Restraint

I therefore urge the United States and the international community to exercise restraint in the face of this daunting challenge. And I urge that this challenge be seen as a global challenge, for terrorism affects all nations, large and small.

I also urge all people of goodwill to recall the wise words of Dr Martin Luther King, Jr, who said that hate, like cancer, "begets hate and violence begets violence in a never-ending circle of destruction."

In the aftermath of this heinous crime, there is the risk that specific communities, such as the Muslims, will face violent repercussions; Islamophobia is not, alas, an uncommon form of xenophobia and intolerance. So it must be emphasised that all ordinary Muslims stand together in condemning such acts of terror. Contemporary Muslim societies have been largely shaped by the recent legacy of their colonial subjugation. Yet, despite their often grim social reality, ordinary Muslim men, women and children abhor those who would use violence to air their grievances.

Muslims, Christians and Jews have a common shared history. The politics of the Middle East must not be allowed to destroy the natural capacity that people of faith have to live together and to work together. We must always hold fast to the moral values contained in our common heritage despite the conflicting rights and comparable injustices still separating us. Bloodshed is no answer.

> "Although tit-for-tat measures may sometimes appear to be an attractive option in the short term, we in the Middle East know that they only make a mockery of any and all attempts at real peace."

An Interconnected World

Tuesday's tragic events serve to remind us that the world today is increasingly interconnected. And as borders come to lose their meaning, no nation can afford to isolate itself. We are moving toward a single world with a single agenda and that agenda must be set with a view to fostering reconciliation and understanding.

Although tit-for-tat measures may sometimes appear to be an attractive option in the short-term, we in the Middle East know that they only make a mockery of any and all attempts at real peace—between traditions, between nations, between civilisations, between equals. We ourselves have failed to develop a civilised framework for disagreement. Sometimes, too, we reject international processes that just might allow us to find a new way forward. This is a mistake and one that must not be repeated in the context of the struggle against terrorism.

A common consensus must be reached to strengthen UN Security Council Resolutions encouraging international cooperation against terrorist activities. Our goal will be to tighten the noose around terrorist networks

In response to the 9/11 terrorist attacks, Jordan's prince El Hassan bin Talal stressed consensus and interconnectedness in the modern world. (Toru Yamanaka/ AFP/Getty Images.)

and their supporters. World leaders and religious representatives across the globe must also send out a clear message that terrorism is anathema to any religion and must be isolated from it.

As we contemplate, in the days and weeks ahead, the horrific images of devastation now etched in our memories and share the grief of our neighbours in the United States, we will also search for other ways to reinforce our common humanity and identify our common fears. For make no mistake about it: Yesterday's attacks were aimed at one world composed of many nations and not at one nation alone.

The U.S. President Addresses the People After 9/11

George W. Bush

In the following speech to Congress and the people of the United States, President George W. Bush acknowledges America's courage in response to the events of 9/11. The attacks, he claims, are an act of war, and he identifies any nation that harbors terrorists an enemy of the United States. Bush demands that the Taliban regime in Afghanistan turn over the leaders of the al Qaeda terrorist network, or face decisive military action, and he calls on the free nations of the world to join in the fight against terrorism. He asks the American people not to single out Arab-Americans or those of the Muslim faith. Bush also asks that Americans cooperate with law enforcement and be patient with tighter security measures. He promises not to forget the attacks and to work tirelessly to wage a war against those who threaten the freedom and security of all Americans.

SOURCE. George W. Bush, "Address to Joint Session of Congress on the 9/11 Attacks," September 20, 2001. PresidentialRhetoric.com.

M embers of Congress and fellow Americans:
In the normal course of events, Presidents come to this chamber to report on the state of the Union. Tonight, no such report is needed. It has already been delivered by the American people.

We have seen it in the courage of passengers, who rushed terrorists to save others on the ground—passengers like an exceptional man named Todd Beamer. And would you please help me to welcome his wife, Lisa Beamer, here tonight [September 20, 2001].

> Whether we bring our enemies to justice, or bring justice to our enemies, justice will be done.

We have seen the state of our Union in the endurance of rescuers, working past exhaustion. We have seen the unfurling of flags, the lighting of candles, the giving of blood, the saying of prayers—in English, Hebrew, and Arabic. We have seen the decency of a loving and giving people who have made the grief of strangers their own.

My fellow citizens, for the last nine days, the entire world has seen for itself the state of our Union—and it is strong.

Tonight we are a country awakened to danger and called to defend freedom. Our grief has turned to anger, and anger to resolution. Whether we bring our enemies to justice, or bring justice to our enemies, justice will be done.

I thank the Congress for its leadership at such an important time. All of America was touched on the evening of the tragedy to see Republicans and Democrats joined together on the steps of this Capitol, singing "God Bless America." And you did more than sing; you acted, by delivering $40 billion to rebuild our communities and meet the needs of our military. . . .

And on behalf of the American people, I thank the world for its outpouring of support. America will never

forget the sounds of our National Anthem playing at Buckingham Palace, on the streets of Paris, and at Berlin's Brandenburg Gate.

We will not forget South Korean children gathering to pray outside our embassy in Seoul, or the prayers of sympathy offered at a mosque in Cairo. We will not forget moments of silence and days of mourning in Australia and Africa and Latin America.

Nor will we forget the citizens of 80 other nations who died with our own: dozens of Pakistanis; more than 130 Israelis; more than 250 citizens of India; men and women from El Salvador, Iran, Mexico, and Japan; and hundreds of British citizens. America has no truer friend than Great Britain. Once again, we are joined together in a great cause—so honored the British Prime Minister [Tony Blair] has crossed an ocean to show his unity of purpose with America. Thank you for coming, friend.

After displaying the badge of a policeman killed in the 9/11 terrorist attacks, U.S. president George W. Bush vowed to "meet violence with patient justice." (Win McNamee/AFP/Getty Images.)

> Americans have known the casualties of war—but not at the center of a great city on a peaceful morning.

The Enemies of Freedom

On September the 11th, enemies of freedom committed an act of war against our country. Americans have known wars—but for the past 136 years, they have been wars on foreign soil, except for one Sunday in 1941. Americans have known the casualties of war—but not at the center of a great city on a peaceful morning. Americans have known surprise attacks—but never before on thousands of civilians. All of this was brought upon us in a single day—and night fell on a different world, a world where freedom itself is under attack.

Americans have many questions tonight. Americans are asking: Who attacked our country? The evidence we have gathered all points to a collection of loosely affiliated terrorist organizations known as al Qaeda. They are the same murderers indicted for bombing American embassies in Tanzania and Kenya, and responsible for bombing the USS *Cole*.

Al Qaeda is to terror what the mafia is to crime. But its goal is not making money; its goal is remaking the world—and imposing its radical beliefs on people everywhere.

The terrorists practice a fringe form of Islamic extremism that has been rejected by Muslim scholars and the vast majority of Muslim clerics—a fringe movement that perverts the peaceful teachings of Islam. The terrorists' directive commands them to kill Christians and Jews, to kill all Americans, and make no distinction among military and civilians, including women and children.

This group and its leader—a person named Osama bin Laden—are linked to many other organizations in different countries, including the Egyptian Islamic Jihad and the Islamic Movement of Uzbekistan. There are thousands of these terrorists in more than 60 countries. They are recruited from their own nations and neighborhoods and brought to camps in places like Afghanistan, where they are trained in the tactics of terror. They are sent back to their homes or sent to hide in countries around the world to plot evil and destruction.

The Taliban Regime

The leadership of al Qaeda has great influence in Afghanistan and supports the Taliban regime in controlling most of that country. In Afghanistan, we see al Qaeda's vision for the world.

Afghanistan's people have been brutalized—many are starving and many have fled. Women are not allowed to attend school. You can be jailed for owning a television. Religion can be practiced only as their leaders dictate. A man can be jailed in Afghanistan if his beard is not long enough.

The United States respects the people of Afghanistan—after all, we are currently its largest source of humanitarian aid—but we condemn the Taliban regime. It is not only repressing its own people, it is threatening people everywhere by sponsoring and sheltering and supplying terrorists. By aiding and abetting murder, the Taliban regime is committing murder.

And tonight, the United States of America makes the following demands on the Taliban: Deliver to United States authorities all the leaders of al Qaeda who hide in your land. Release all foreign nationals, including American citizens, you have unjustly imprisoned. Protect foreign journalists, diplomats, and aid workers in your country. Close immediately and permanently every terrorist training camp in Afghanistan, and hand over every terrorist, and every person in their support structure, to appropriate authorities. Give the United States full access to terrorist training camps, so we can make sure they are no longer operating.

These demands are not open to negotiation or discussion. The Taliban must act, and act immediately. They will hand over the terrorists, or they will share in their fate.

I also want to speak tonight directly to Muslims throughout the world. We respect your faith. It's practiced freely by many millions of Americans, and by millions more in countries that America counts as friends. Its teachings are good and peaceful, and those who commit evil in the name of Allah blaspheme the name of Allah. The terrorists are traitors to their own faith, trying, in effect, to hijack Islam itself. The enemy of America is not our many Muslim friends; it is not our many Arab friends. Our enemy is a radical network of terrorists, and every government that supports them.

> From this day forward, any nation that continues to harbor or support terrorism will be regarded by the United States as a hostile regime.

Our war on terror begins with al Qaeda, but it does not end there. It will not end until every terrorist group of global reach has been found, stopped, and defeated.

Why Do They Hate Us?

Americans are asking, why do they hate us? They hate what we see right here in this chamber—a democratically elected government. Their leaders are self-appointed. They hate our freedoms—our freedom of religion, our freedom of speech, our freedom to vote and assemble and disagree with each other.

They want to overthrow existing governments in many Muslim countries, such as Egypt, Saudi Arabia, and Jordan. They want to drive Israel out of the Middle East. They want to drive Christians and Jews out of vast regions of Asia and Africa.

These terrorists kill not merely to end lives, but to disrupt and end a way of life. With every atrocity, they hope that America grows fearful, retreating from the world and forsaking our friends. They stand against us, because we stand in their way.

We are not deceived by their pretenses to piety. We have seen their kind before. They are the heirs of all the murderous ideologies of the 20th century. By sacrificing human life to serve their radical visions—by abandoning every value except the will to power—they follow in the path of fascism, and Nazism, and totalitarianism. And they will follow that path all the way, to where it ends: in history's unmarked grave of discarded lies.

Americans are asking: How will we fight and win this war? We will direct every resource at our command—every means of diplomacy, every tool of intelligence, every instrument of law enforcement, every financial influence, and every necessary weapon of war—to the disruption and to the defeat of the global terror network.

A War on Terrorism

This war will not be like the war against Iraq a decade ago, with a decisive liberation of territory and a swift conclusion. It will not look like the air war above Kosovo two years ago, where no ground troops were used and not a single American was lost in combat.

Our response involves far more than instant retaliation and isolated strikes. Americans should not expect one battle, but a lengthy campaign, unlike any other we have ever seen. It may include dramatic strikes, visible on TV, and covert operations, secret even in success. We will starve terrorists of funding, turn them one against another, drive them from place to place, until there is no refuge or no rest. And we will pursue nations that provide aid or safe haven to terrorism. Every nation, in every region, now has a decision to make. Either you are with us, or you are with the terrorists. From this day forward, any nation that continues to harbor or support terrorism will be regarded by the United States as a hostile regime.

Our nation has been put on notice: We are not immune from attack. We will take defensive measures against terrorism to protect Americans. Today, dozens of federal departments and agencies, as well as state and local governments, have responsibilities affecting homeland security. These efforts must be coordinated at the highest level. So tonight I announce the creation of a Cabinet-level position reporting directly to me—the Office of Homeland Security.

And tonight I also announce a distinguished American to lead this effort, to strengthen American security: a military veteran, an effective governor, a true patriot, a trusted friend—Pennsylvania's Tom Ridge. He will lead, oversee, and coordinate a comprehensive national strategy to safeguard our country against terrorism, and respond to any attacks that may come.

These measures are essential. But the only way to defeat terrorism as a threat to our way of life is to stop it, eliminate it, and destroy it where it grows.

Many will be involved in this effort, from FBI agents to intelligence operatives to the reservists we have called to active duty. All deserve our thanks, and all have our prayers. And tonight, a few miles from the damaged Pentagon, I have a message for our military: Be ready. I've called the Armed Forces to alert, and there is a reason. The hour is coming when America will act, and you will make us proud.

The World's Fight

This is not, however, just America's fight. And what is at stake is not just America's freedom. This is the world's fight. This is civilization's fight. This is the fight of all who believe in progress and pluralism, tolerance and freedom.

We ask every nation to join us. We will ask, and we will need, the help of police forces, intelligence services, and banking systems around the world. The United

States is grateful that many nations and many international organizations have already responded—with sympathy and with support. Nations from Latin America, to Asia, to Africa, to Europe, to the Islamic world. Perhaps the NATO [North Atlantic Treaty Organization] Charter reflects best the attitude of the world: An attack on one is an attack on all.

The civilized world is rallying to America's side. They understand that if this terror goes unpunished, their own cities, their own citizens may be next. Terror, unanswered, can not only bring down buildings, it can threaten the stability of legitimate governments. And you know what—we're not going to allow it.

What Can Americans Do?

Americans are asking: What is expected of us? I ask you to live your lives, and hug your children. I know many citizens have fears tonight, and I ask you to be calm and resolute, even in the face of a continuing threat. I ask you to uphold the values of America, and remember why so many have come here. We are in a fight for our principles, and our first responsibility is to live by them. No one should be singled out for unfair treatment or unkind words because of their ethnic background or religious faith. . . .

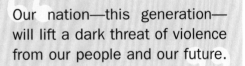

Our nation—this generation—will lift a dark threat of violence from our people and our future.

The thousands of FBI agents who are now at work in this investigation may need your cooperation, and I ask you to give it.

I ask for your patience, with the delays and inconveniences that may accompany tighter security; and for your patience in what will be a long struggle.

I ask your continued participation and confidence in the American economy. Terrorists attacked a symbol of American prosperity. They did not touch its source. America is successful because of the hard work, and creativity, and enterprise of our people. These were the true strengths of our economy before September 11th, and they are our strengths today.

And, finally, please continue praying for the victims of terror and their families, for those in uniform, and for our great country. Prayer has comforted us in sorrow, and will help strengthen us for the journey ahead.

Coming Together

Tonight I thank my fellow Americans for what you have already done and for what you will do. And ladies and gentlemen of the Congress, I thank you, their representatives, for what you have already done and for what we will do together.

Tonight we face new and sudden national challenges. We will come together to improve air safety, to dramatically expand the number of air marshals on domestic flights, and take new measures to prevent hijacking. We will come together to promote stability and keep our airlines flying, with direct assistance during this emergency.

We will come together to give law enforcement the additional tools it needs to track down terror here at home. We will come together to strengthen our intelligence capabilities to know the plans of terrorists before they act, and find them before they strike.

We will come together to take active steps that strengthen America's economy, and put our people back to work.

Tonight we welcome two leaders who embody the extraordinary spirit of all New Yorkers: Governor George Pataki, and Mayor Rudolph Giuliani. As a symbol of America's resolve, my administration will work with Congress, and these two leaders, to show the world that we will rebuild New York City.

After all that has just passed—all the lives taken, and all the possibilities and hopes that died with them—it is natural to wonder if America's future is one of fear. Some speak of an age of terror. I know there are struggles ahead, and dangers to face. But this country will define our times, not be defined by them. As long as the United States of America is determined and strong, this will not be an age of terror; this will be an age of liberty, here and across the world.

Great harm has been done to us. We have suffered great loss. And in our grief and anger we have found our mission and our moment. Freedom and fear are at war. The advance of human freedom—the great achievement of our time, and the great hope of every time—now depends on us. Our nation—this generation—will lift a dark threat of violence from our people and our future. We will rally the world to this cause by our efforts, by our courage. We will not tire, we will not falter, and we will not fail.

It is my hope that in the months and years ahead, life will return almost to normal. We'll go back to our lives and routines, and that is good. Even

> I will not relent in waging this struggle for freedom and security for the American people.

grief recedes with time and grace. But our resolve must not pass. Each of us will remember what happened that day, and to whom it happened. We'll remember the moment the news came—where we were and what we were doing. Some will remember an image of a fire, or a story of rescue. Some will carry memories of a face and a voice gone forever.

And I will carry this: It is the police shield of a man named George Howard, who died at the World Trade Center trying to save others. It was given to me by his mom, Arlene, as a proud memorial to her son. This is my reminder of lives that ended, and a task that does not end.

I will not forget this wound to our country or those who inflicted it. I will not yield; I will not rest; I will not relent in waging this struggle for freedom and security for the American people.

The course of this conflict is not known, yet its outcome is certain. Freedom and fear, justice and cruelty, have always been at war, and we know that God is not neutral between them.

Fellow citizens, we'll meet violence with patient justice—assured of the rightness of our cause, and confident of the victories to come. In all that lies before us, may God grant us wisdom, and may He watch over the United States of America.

The Painful Process of Dealing with the Dead

Richard Bernstein and the staff of the *New York Times*

Most of those who died when the World Trade Center (WTC) collapsed were never found, forcing surviving families to make heartbreaking decisions. In the following excerpt from *Out of the Blue*, a book by Richard Bernstein and the staff of the *New York Times*, the author examines some of the problems that families of the dead face. For example, the Buddhist funeral ceremony requires that the family pass around the cremated bones of the deceased, but Kazushige Ito, a victim of the WTC collapse, left no body behind. The authors explain that some families postponed burials, fearing the bodies had been misidentified, while others were waiting for the discovery of more body parts. Family members of those who died on Flight 93, which crashed in Pennsylvania, had the advantage of knowing what happened, but the authors explain that without bodies, families of missing WTC victims suffered the pain of hope and despair over and over again.

SOURCE. Richard Bernstein, *Out of the Blue*. New York: Times Books/Henry Holt, 2002. Copyright © 2002 by Richard Bernstein. All rights reserved. Reproduced by permission of Henry Holt and Company, LLC. and the author.

The funeral for Kazushige Ito, a thirty-five-year-old planning specialist at Fuji Bank, took place in that famously afflicted city, Hiroshima, Japan, on March 9, 2002, six months after Ito died in the south tower of the World Trade Center. Ito's father, Tsugio Ito, spoke at the ceremony, and there must have been an added measure of sadness for him, if it is possible for anything to add to the sadness of attending the funeral of a son without a body to put to rest. In the usual Buddhist ceremony of Japan, relatives meet in the crematorium and they use chopsticks to pick the cremated bones out of the ash and pass them from person to person. But this was the second time in Tsugio Ito's life when a funeral was held without the body being placed on an altar so that the sutras can be intoned by the priest, and without incense being sprinkled on the smoldering remains. The older Ito's older brother, the uncle that Kazushige never met, died many years ago at another ground zero. He was vaporized when the atomic bomb was dropped there on August 6, 1945. In both cases the grief of the Ito family was intensified by the deaths of young men in events so cataclysmic they left behind no trace of the deceased.

> [Kazushige Ito's] remains are still there at Ground Zero in New York in what became a common mass grave.

"What happened in Hiroshima and in the terrorism [in New York] is the same because there are many people who can't recover one tooth or one nail," Ito told a Japanese reporter.

Kazushige Ito was a music lover who used to go to the Metropolitan Opera House at Lincoln Center in New York twenty times in a season. He was also a marathoner who finished the New York City event in four hours eighteen minutes in 2000 and was jogging every day in Central Park to get ready for the Philadelphia Marathon, which he planned to run in November. His goal was to break the four-hour mark, and his wife,

Yuko, said she believed he would have done it. He would have turned thirty-six the day after the Philadelphia Marathon, if he had lived. If he had lived, he would probably have settled permanently in New York, a city both he and Yuko loved.

But he didn't live. He was probably one of those killed when flight 175 plowed into the south tower at 9:02 on September 11, since Fuji Bank was one of the unfortunate companies whose offices were at the immediate point of impact. Maybe Kazushige Ito was one of those who heeded the public address announcements ordering people not to evacuate the south tower after the north tower was hit and that is why he was sitting at his desk when Marwan al-Shehhi slammed the hijacked Boeing 767 into his office on the 81st floor, killing sixty-two Fuji Bank employees altogether. Stanley Praimnath, who walked out of the south tower with Brian Clark, did survive the crash on the 81st floor. He also worked at Fuji Bank, and he may have been the only person who was on the 81st floor who survived.

In any case, Kazushige Ito is dead, though his body was never recovered. His remains are still there at Ground Zero in New York in what became a common mass grave. His father visited the site in October, and he remembers feeling for the members of the rescue and cleanup crews who, he felt, were freezing in the late autumn weather. He remembers also going to the bathroom to weep privately over his loss. Eventually he gave up on finding Kazushige's body, saying that everybody was doing the best they could. And in March, finally, a funeral service was held at which Ito addressed the spirit of his son directly:

> Most of the dead were never found and never will be.

"Please look after us from heaven," he said. "And don't worry. I'm thinking about making a new start today." . . .

Memorials and shrines for the dead helped some 9/11 survivors cope with the lack of human remains left by the attacks. (**AP Images.**)

Most of the dead were never found and never will be, which is one of the matters that makes the redevelopment of the Trade Center site in lower Manhattan so delicate a matter. It is hallowed ground and it is a commercial site. And, as always in matters of disaster, September 11 was followed by a debate about practical matters, legal disputes between the leaseholder and the consortium that insured the towers—for $3.5 billion or $7 billion, depending on whether the attack is considered a single event or two separate events. There were arguments about an appropriate memorial to the dead; there were demonstrations by firefighters who scuffled with police after Mayor Guiliani, one of the heroes of the day, decided in late October that the search for remains would have to end and the cleanup begin. An enormous out-pouring of generosity followed the disaster, with dona-tions pouring by the millions into the coffers of charities and relief organizations, but even that brought its dark side as quarrels erupted over when the money would be distributed, and how much. And then, of course, in the days right after the tragedy, the United States went on a war footing with President Bush warning the govern-ments that had harbored terrorists, most notably the Taliban government of Afghanistan, that they would be treated as terrorists themselves.

In New York the mourning went on, and so did the many private struggles of the bereaved to come to accept the bitter fact, as Tsugio Ito was forced to do, that their missing loved ones were not going to turn up alive. By the first week of October, only 321 remains had been identified of the thousands who were missing. Mayor Giuliani himself went to the city morgue to identify the remains of Terence S. Hatton, a fire captain who was married to a longtime may-oral aide. A team of people, police officers, Fire Department battalion chiefs, clergymen, and others, were

> After six months . . . 18,937 body parts and 287 whole bod-ies had been found in the rub-ble, and 972 identifications had been made—which meant that there was no trace yet of 1,852 victims.

enlisted to go to the homes of the identified victims to give the news that a body had been found directly and in person. Members of some three thousand families gave DNA samples, toothbrushes, razors, even lip balm used by victims, and saliva swabs from the victims' relatives, to help in the work of identification, with DNA collection kits sent away to places like Germany and Guatemala where some of the bereaved families lived. And whenever a match was made—sometimes from nothing more than a fragment of bone found in the debris—there would be that visit to a family informing them that something had been found proving their loved one's decease, and at least the suspense and anguish of waiting would be over.

Inevitably this process entailed some heartbreaking bureaucratic formalities. Families were required to fill out forms in which they specified what they wanted to do if additional tissue samples of a loved one were found. There were two choices: they could be notified or they could have the sample disposed of by the authorities. Exactly how the disposal of what the printed form did not call body parts was to be done was not specified.

"When you get that knock on the door, it's the big one," said Michael Meehan, a New York City detective whose brother, Damian Meehan, a trader at Carr Futures, was among those whose bodies were identified in the wreckage.

After six months, a set of grisly statistics were announced in the cool language of bureaucracy. To that date, 18,937 body parts and 287 whole bodies had been found in the rubble, and 972 identifications had been made—which meant that there was no trace yet of 1,852 victims. Only two of the sixty-five people (not including the hijackers) aboard flight 175 were identified, which is no doubt an index of the incinerating heat that accompanied their deaths. By contrast, 182 of the firemen, who wore protective gear, have been identified, out of the total of 343 dead. But almost all of the remains were burned or mangled beyond recognition. The identities of only ten victims were confirmed by visual identification alone. All the rest were done through dental records, fingerprints, and, above all, by DNA testing.

Families faced heartbreaking choices that sometimes even the most well-designed bureaucratic procedures could only make worse. Do you bury a part of a body and hold a funeral, or do you wait in the hopes that more of the body will be found? What if you have a funeral without a body and then the medical examiner calls to tell you months later that a body was found? Do you have another funeral, or just a burial or a cremation? If only part of a body is found, do you bury it in a full-sized coffin or in some smaller container? And, if you have buried what was initially found of a body and more is found later, do you disinter the original remains and rebury them with the newly found parts? And if your loved one is found mangled almost beyond recognition, or if you are only burying parts of a body, do you view the remains? Painful as it sounds, many counselors recommended that the remains be viewed on the grounds that it might help in accepting the tragedy that had occurred, in providing what is commonly called closure.

Beata Boyarski, twenty-five, whose thirty-four-year-old brother Gennady Boyarski's body was found in the rubble, called the medical examiner in an effort to be sure that the body had not been misidentified. In her grief she entertained the suspicion that the city might just be trying to get rid of bodies without worrying excessively about who they belonged to.

'So many people don't know what happened, but I do know. I had the phone calls. I heard the black box.'

"Tell me like it is," she said to the medical examiner, whom she managed to get on the phone. The body was horribly mangled, the medical examiner told her, and only about three-quarters of it had been found, along with a wedding ring and a wallet. The identification was made from a driver's license and the cause of death was given as "blunt impact," which provided Ms. Boyarski with no information about how Gennady, who left behind a wife and a seven-year-old son, had died and where exactly and at what time. When Ms. Boyarski said that the family wanted DNA testing done just to be sure of the identification, she was told that that might take several months, so she went ahead with a burial, only to be told when it was already too late that the DNA testing could be done right away after all. If further remains were found, she said, "We would, I guess, bring him back up and include it." . . .

Susan Rescorla watched on television as the second tower crumbled into dust and she ran out of her house and into the street, and there she saw one of her neighbors, a woman whose husband was at a meeting on the 100th floor, do the same thing. It seems to have been a terror reflex, the impulse to get away from the television screen with its images of horror.

"From that moment on, for the whole day, and for the next week, we held vigil," she said later. Despite her hopes, Rick didn't come home that night, and he didn't call, and she was, of course, fearful that the worst had happened, even as she wanted to cling to some hope that it hadn't. "We did everything to find him," she said of herself and her two daughters. "Unfortunately, because of the chaotic situation there was a lot of misinformation. Hospitals were saying that people were on a list when they weren't. We got one report that somebody had seen him, but it must have been somebody who saw him inside the building. For one second we thought maybe he had gotten out, but he hadn't. We hoped that maybe he was walking around someplace in a daze, and then, at the end of a week, we understood there was no hope." . . .

On April 19, 2002, the FBI allowed the relatives of people killed on flight 93 into a large conference room in Princeton, New Jersey, so they could hear the plane's cockpit voice recorder. For months the federal government had denied the families' requests to do that, on the grounds that, first, the tape was confused and jumbled and didn't hold any answers to the plane's crash in Pennsylvania, and, second, that the tape would be used in evidence in the upcoming trial of Zacarias Moussaoui, and was therefore protected by judicial secrecy. But the families persisted, and they were invited to hear the tape, though they first had to sign a waiver promising not to sue the government in any matter connected to it. About a hundred people, according to one estimate, sat in the conference room. They listened to the tape on headsets installed at each seat, and they watched a written transcript on a large screen in front of them.

The family members' comments on the tape confirmed earlier press reports about them. Shouts of "Get them, get them" could be heard, and so could somebody saying in Arabic, "They're trying to get in." An unidentified woman could be heard saying, "Oh God, Oh God." But the basic questions—Did the passengers actually get into the cockpit? Did the struggle with the hijackers cause the plane to crash, or did the hijackers crash, or blow up, the plane intentionally?—were not resolved. And there were no answers about what role any given person played.

"I didn't hear anything that indicated what my son had done," Jerry Guadagno, the father of Richard Guadagno, said later. "There was really nothing there. I guess the big question mark still remains, and it always will."

Lyz Glick went to the tape playing also, and she is convinced that it does prove the success of the passengers in breaking into the cabin. What else would all that shouting and commotion mean, she wonders.

"But when it came to the last two minutes, which is just the sound of the wind in the cockpit, I stopped listening," she said. "I started shaking. I'm glad I listened to it, but I knew how much I could listen."

At least, she feels, she knows what happened to Jeremy, and she was connected to him in his final minutes, and she knows that, in its way, that was a rare privilege among the survivors of the victims of September 11.

"In a way it does make things a little easier," she said. "So many people don't know what

> Very few, if any, people whose relatives were missing in the hours after the attack turned up alive in hospitals later.

happened, but I do know. I had the phone calls. I heard the black box." . . .

Like many people, Brian Clark went to a lot of funerals after September 11. He went to the funeral of Bobbie Coll, whom he last saw walking up the stairs, the wrong direction, helping the heavy woman who had told them they couldn't go down. He went to the funeral of Jose Marreno, the man who he saw on the 68th floor and who walked back upstairs to help a colleague. In the week right after the disaster, he spent a lot of time answering the phone calls of people who were still hoping that their missing relatives might yet be alive. They asked him if he had seen them, and if he had spoken to them, and whether he thought they might have made it out safely.

> By April [2002], the mountain of debris had essentially disappeared, carted away truckload by truckload and sifted for human remains.

"I couldn't help them, but I would tell them that they had to remain hopeful," he said. "I didn't want to dash their hopes but you had to be realistic as well."

Very few, if any, people whose relatives were missing in the hours after the attack turned up alive in hospitals later. After a week or so, like Susan Rescorla, most relatives realized that there was no hope.

Clark himself got a new job at Euro Brokers. He became president of the Euro Brokers Relief Fund, Inc., whose purpose is to raise money to help the families of the sixty-one Euro Brokers employees who died. About eight months after September 11, he had raised about $3 million. More than $1 million came in from a Charity Day that the company announced, a day on which 100 percent of the revenues—revenues, not profits—went into the fund, a total of about $1.2 million. Other money came from donations, including donations from both Euro Brokers customers and competitors.

"It's sort of an endless process," Clark said. "There are children who will have needs going into the future, medical insurance needs, education needs, whatever they are."

While friends and relatives of the victims mourned and faced the future, the cleanup at Ground Zero continued, and the authorities set up a viewing stand on the corner of Fulton Street and Broadway where people could go to look at the scene. You had to get a ticket at the South Street Seaport and you walked up a ramp—the ancient, sycamore-shaded graveyard of St. Paul's Church was on the right—to the platform itself, where you had the right to a half hour on the stand itself before a man in a blue jacket with the inscription "NYPD Community Affairs" politely urged you to leave.

By April, the mountain of debris had essentially disappeared, carted away truckload by truckload and sifted for human remains. Standing on the viewing stand, which looked east to west, you could see the foundations of the towers, surrounded on one side by the largely unscathed World Financial Center buildings across West Street, and several other skyscrapers still draped in netting. It no longer looked like a disaster site; it looked like a construction site, with all those rows of sheds you see in such places on the street level alongside an immense excavated rectangle.

Near the entrance ramp, visitors by the thousands had left small mementos—fire department hats from across the country, T-shirts, banners, pictures of victims, prayers scrawled on squares of cloth or on the plywood sheets that served as partitions for the viewing stand. Most of all, people just wrote their names, tens of thousands of them, and the places they had come from, or they left a little message: "Arkansas prays for you," or "The Smiths are so soorry," with sorry spelled incorrectly, or "God Bless All of You," or "Aspire and Persevere." There were some obscenities as well, directed mostly at Osama bin Laden. There was what looked a bit like corporate sponsorship: "Southwest Airlines Loves NYC."

On the exit ramp was a large plaque, hung on a plywood partition, with the names of many of the victims, those who had died on flights 11 and 175 and those who had died in the north and south towers inscribed alphabetically. The framed plaque was festooned with flags, with roses, rosary beads, and pictures of victims. Nearby was a poster saying, "Imagine—a Department of Peace." The spire of St. John's Church, converted into a hospitality room reserved for rescue workers, soared above. On the plaque, which ran for perhaps thirty feet, was an inscription, the final sentence of the letter that Abraham Lincoln wrote to Mrs. Bixby of Massachusetts who lost her five sons, all she had, on the battlefields of the Civil War. Lincoln's letter was written for a very different circumstance, and yet, in its lean elegance, it seemed entirely suitable to soothe the afflicted spirits of those whose loved ones were taken from them on September 11:

"I pray that our heavenly Father may assuage the anguish of your bereavement, and leave you only with the cherished memory of the loved and lost, and the solemn pride that must be yours to have laid so costly a sacrifice upon the altar of freedom."

CHAPTER 2

The Controversies Surrounding 9/11

U.S. Intelligence Failures Made the United States Vulnerable on 9/11

Amy B. Zegart

Most Americans now know that important intelligence did not make its way to the right agencies in time to prevent the terrorist attacks of 9/11. In the following viewpoint, excerpted from her book *Spying Blind*, UCLA professor and intelligence expert Amy B. Zegart argues that blaming intelligence failures on individuals does not get to the root of the problem. She claims that organizational problems better explain why U.S. intelligence agencies failed to prevent the 9/11 attacks. Zegart maintains, for example, that counterterrorism efforts were not only underfunded, but also scattered among forty-six different agencies. Moreover, she asserts that these agencies remained trapped in Cold War priorities and procedures and resisted using new ideas and technologies. Rather than blame individual leadership, policy makers should address systemic failures, Zegart reasons.

Photo on previous page: Opinions differed on how best to respond to the 9/11 attacks, and on how best to prevent similar events. (Eric Feferberg/ AFP/Getty Images.)

SOURCE. Amy B. Zegart, *Spying Blind: the CIA, the FBI, and the Origins of 9/11*. Copyright © 2007 by Princeton University Press. Reprinted by permission of Princeton University Press.

In January 2000, al Qaeda operatives from around the world gathered secretly in Malaysia for a planning meeting. The Central Intelligence Agency (CIA) was watching. Among the participants was a man named Khalid al-Mihdhar, one of the September 11 hijackers who would later help to crash American Airlines Flight 77 into the Pentagon. By the time the meeting disbanded, the CIA had taken a photograph of al-Mihdhar, learned his full name, obtained his passport number, and uncovered one other critical piece of information: al-Mihdhar held a multiple-entry visa to the United States. It was twenty months before the September 11, 2001, terrorist attacks on the World Trade Center and Pentagon. George Tenet, the director of central intelligence (DCI), later admitted that the CIA should have immediately placed al-Mihdhar on the State Department's watch list denying him entry into the United States, and it should have notified other government agencies such as the FBI. But the CIA did not do so until August 23, 2001, just nineteen days before the attacks and months after al-Mihdhar had entered the country, obtained a California motor vehicle photo identification card—using his real name—and started taking flying lessons.

> Evidence suggests . . . that the right information did not get to the right places at the right time.

Looking for Answers

The case of Khalid al-Mihdhar provides a chilling example of the subtle yet powerful effects of organization— that is, the cultures, incentives, and structures that critically influence what government agencies do and how well they do it. Why did the CIA take so long to put this suspected al Qaeda operative on the State Department's watch list, especially given Director Tenet's earlier declaration that the United States was "at war" with al Qaeda, his clear public warnings to Congress—for three consecutive years—that Osama bin Laden was determined to strike major blows against American targets, and when intelligence chatter about preparations for a "spectacular" attack was spiking in the spring and summer of 2001?

The simplest answer is that the agency had never been in the habit of watch listing al Qaeda operatives before. For more than forty years, the Central Intelligence Agency and the twelve other agencies of the U.S. Intelligence Community (IC) had operated with Cold War procedures, priorities, and thinking, all of which had little need for making sure foreign terrorists stayed out of the United States. Before September 11, there was no formal training program, no well-honed process, and no sustained level of attention given to ensuring that intelligence officers would identify dangerous terrorists and warn other U.S. government agencies about them before they reached the United States. As one CIA employee told congressional investigators after the September 11 attacks, he believed it was "not incumbent" even on the CIA's special Osama bin Laden unit to place people such as al-Mihdhar on the State Department's watch list.

No one will ever know whether the World Trade Center and Pentagon attacks could have been prevented. Evidence suggests, however, that the right information did not get to the right places at the right time. Many of the agonizing missteps and missed clues have been widely publicized. There is the star Phoenix FBI agent who warned in a July 2001 memo that Osama bin Laden could be training terrorists in U.S. flight schools, a warning that never made it to the top of the FBI or a single other intelligence agency. There is the refusal by FBI headquarters to seek a search warrant for the computer files of Zacarias Moussaoui, a foreign flight school student who Minneapolis field agents were convinced was plotting a terrorist attack with a large aircraft and who later became the only person convicted in the United States for his connection to the 9/11 attacks. And there is the president's August 6, 2001, CIA briefing entitled "Bin Laden Determined to Strike in U.S.," which gave the impression the

> "Counterterrorism efforts were as scattered as they were underfunded, split among forty-six different agencies."

FBI had the threat covered, erroneously suggested that Yemen tourists taking photographs were terrorists casing federal buildings in New York, and made no mention of crucial pieces of information that should have been pursued aggressively. These included the Phoenix memo, the al Qaeda summit in Malaysia, al-Mihdhar's U.S. visa, and the CIA's discovery that a second September 11 hijacker who had attended the summit, Nawaf al-Hazmi, had also entered the United States. Thanks to the extraordinary work of the 9/11 Commission and the House and Senate Intelligence Committees' Joint Inquiry into the attacks, most Americans have a good idea of what went wrong in the weeks and months before September 11. The challenge now is to explain *why* it went wrong. . . .

Failing to Adapt

The answer lies in organizations, more specifically, in the deeply rooted organizational weaknesses that have afflicted U.S. intelligence agencies for decades and in the enduring impediments to fixing them. The single most important reason the United States remained so vulnerable on September 11 was not the McDonald's wages paid to airport security workers, the Clinton administration's inability to capture or kill Osama bin Laden, or the Bush administration's failure to place terrorism higher on its priority list. It was the stunning inability of U.S. intelligence agencies to adapt to the end of the Cold War.

During the 1990s, for example, intelligence officials repeatedly warned of a grave and growing terrorist threat even while they continued old funding patterns that favored electronic surveillance—ideal for counting Soviet warheads—over human intelligence efforts better suited for penetrating terrorist groups. Although details about U.S. intelligence spending are classified, conservative estimates based on the declassified 1997 intelligence budget put annual human intelligence spending at $1.6 billion, a little more than the cost of building and launching a single spy satellite. The amount of money spent directly to support human intelligence operations in the field was even less. As one official with access to the CIA's human intelligence budget put it, once pensions, salaries, and other expenses were paid, "The James Bond fund that people think we're doing came down to $500 million," or less than 2 percent of the annual intelligence budget at the time.

Scattered Efforts

Counterterrorism efforts were as scattered as they were underfunded, split among forty-six different agencies without a central strategy, budget, or coordinating mechanism. Director of Central Intelligence George Tenet declared war on Osama bin Laden in a December 1998 memo and urged that "no resources or people [be] spared" to fight him, but proved unable to mass his troops in the right places. Although Tenet tried to increase dramatically the size of the Counterterrorist Center, he failed, leaving only five analysts assigned to Osama bin Laden on September 11.

The CIA was not alone. The FBI formally declared terrorism its number one priority as early as 1998. Yet on September 11, 2001, only 6 percent of FBI personnel were working on counterterrorism issues, new agents still received more time for vacation than counterterrorism training, and the vast majority of the FBI's intelligence analysts—precisely the people who were charged with connecting the dots across different FBI cases—were found to be unqualified to perform their jobs. Steeped in an eighty-year-old culture that prized searching houses more than searching databases, the agency lacked basic computer capabilities to see whether the words "flight training school" showed up in any of its case files and

Lapses by the FBI left the 9/11 plotters undeterred in their actions against the United States. (Roberto Schmidt/AFP/Getty Images.)

even the FBI Director, Louis Freeh, ordered the computer removed from his office because he never used it. In the words of one FBI official, the prevailing attitude was, "real men don't type. The only thing a real agent needs is a notebook, a pen, and a gun, and with those three things you can conquer the world." Just weeks before the attacks, a highly classified internal review of the bureau's counterterrorism capabilities gave failing grades to every one of the FBI's fifty-six U.S. field offices.

Core Organizational Weaknesses

These problems were not isolated mistakes, failures of foresight, or the result of poor decisions by individuals asleep at the switch. Instead, they were symptoms of three deeper and more intractable organizational deficiencies: (1) cultural pathologies that led intelligence agencies to resist new technologies, ideas, and tasks; (2) perverse promotion incentives that rewarded intelligence officials for all of the wrong things; and (3) structural weaknesses dating back decades that hindered the operation of the CIA and FBI and prevented the U.S. Intelligence Community from working as a coherent whole. It was these core weaknesses that caused U.S. intelligence agencies to blow key operational opportunities—such as watch listing al-Mihdhar or searching Zacarias Mousssaoui's computer files—that might have disrupted the September 11 plot. And it was these core weaknesses that kept U.S. intelligence agencies from getting more chances to defeat al Qaeda in the first place. With FBI agents keeping case files in shoe boxes rather than putting them into computers, with CIA operatives clinging to old systems designed for recruiting Soviet officials at cocktail parties rather than Jihadists in caves, with career incentives that rewarded intelligence officials for staying cloistered in their own agencies rather than working across agency lines, and with a forty-year-old intelligence structure that gave no person the power to match resources against priorities and knock bureau-cratic heads together, the U.S. Intelligence Community did not have a fighting chance against al Qaeda.

The existence of these organiza-tional deficiencies, and the urgent need to fix them, was no secret in Washington before the September 11 attacks. Between 1991 and 2001, intelligence problems and counter-terrorism challenges were the subject of at least six classified reports and a dozen major unclassified studies. The unclassified stud-ies alone issued more than 500 recommendations for reform across the U.S. government. Two-thirds of these recommendations, or 340 in total, targeted the CIA, FBI, and the rest of the U.S. Intelligence Community. Yet only 35 of these 340 intelligence recommendations were successfully implemented before September 11, and most—268 to be exact—resulted in no action what-soever. In January 2001, nine months before the attacks, the bipartisan blue-ribbon Hart-Rudman Commission offered the most comprehensive assessment of U.S. national security challenges and deficiencies since World War II. The commission issued stark conclusions: "the dramatic changes in the world since the end of the Cold War," it noted, "have not been accompanied by any major institutional changes in the Executive branch of the U.S. government." The commission presciently predicted that institutional deficiencies left the United States homeland exceptionally vulnerable to catastrophic terrorist attack.

No system is failure-proof. As Richard Betts wrote in *Foreign Affairs* shortly after September 11, "The awful truth is that even the best intelligence systems will have big failures." Evidence suggests, however, that U.S. intelligence agencies were nowhere close to being the best before 9/11, and that they could have been better.

> "Institutional deficiencies left the United States homeland exceptionally vulnerable to catastrophic terrorist attack."

When the Soviet Union fell in 1991 and the principal threat to U.S. national security changed, the Intelligence Community was slow to change with it.

The Finger Pointing Fallacy

> Highlighting the role of individuals is . . . dangerous because it suggests the wrong causes of failure and the wrong remedies to address them.

Why? What is it that prevented the CIA, the FBI, and other agencies from adapting to the rising terrorist threat during the 1990s? To date, no one has provided satisfying answers. Academics have avoided the subject, concentrating instead on research topics that have more readily available data, fit more squarely into existing theories, and do not require delving into the controversial business of spying. At the same time, politicians and journalists have preferred to point fingers, focusing on who failed to do what and when. The result is a prevailing wisdom that mistakenly attributes the failures of September 11 to individuals. . . .

Highlighting the role of individuals is . . . dangerous because it suggests the wrong causes of failure and the wrong remedies to address them. We are left to think that if only the right people had been heard, if only a few important officials had connected a few obvious dots, if only more leaders inside the corridors of power had had their hair on fire, tragedy could have been averted. As Bob Woodward, the dean of journalist nonfiction, once wrote, "Decision making at the highest levels of national government is a complex human interaction. . . . This human story is the core."

The Unexamined Causes

Actually, the human story is the problem. What is missing from these accounts is a sense of context, the underlying constraints and forces that make it likely talented people will make poor decisions. It is easy, for example, to blame intelligence officials for overlooking warnings about a terrorist attack in an intercepted telephone conversation. It is much harder when one considers that several million such conversations are intercepted by intelligence officials every day of every week of every year. Journalists, the old saying goes, write the first draft of history. In the case of September 11, however, journalists have provided the *only* draft of history. The fault is not theirs, but ours in the academy: political scientists have devoted almost no attention to studying U.S. intelligence since 9/11. The result is that the role of individuals in September 11 has been grossly overstated, while the organizational causes of failure have gone largely unexamined. . . .

> Individuals made mistakes, but it was the system that failed us.

My point is not that individual leadership never matters, but that the harder-to-see aspects of organizational life—such as training, procedures, cultures, and agency structures—often matter more. This is important, both for our understanding of the past and our expectations of the future. Indeed, if individual leadership determined counterterrorism success and failure, then fixing U.S. intelligence agencies would be easy. One need only identify the few bad apples and toss, or vote, them out. The reality is much worse. Yes, individuals made mistakes, but it was the system that failed us.

U.S. Cultural Excess and Foreign Policy Breed Discontent Among Would-Be Terrorists

Riad Z. Abdelkarim

Following the 9/11 attacks, many Americans asked, why do the terrorists hate us? In the following viewpoint, Dr. Riad Z. Abdelkarim, communications director for the Council on American-Islamic Relations, offers his perspective. He argues that the question is misleading. Most Muslims, he maintains, do not hate the United States and, in fact, are often envious of the freedoms available to U.S. Muslims. Abdelkarim asserts, however, that the U.S. culture promoted by Hollywood appears excessive and materialistic to conservative Muslims. Moreover, he reasons, U.S. foreign policies, such as the support of oppressive leaders and Israel's treatment of Palestinians, cre-

SOURCE. Riad Z. Abdelkarim, "Why Do They Hate Us?" *Washington Report on Middle East Affairs*, vol. 21, March 1, 2002, p. 84. Copyright © 2002 American Educational Trust. All rights reserved. Reproduced by permission.

ate discontent and resentment among those Muslims who have been disenfranchised by these policies.

One of the most widely asked questions in the weeks and months following the Sept. 11 terrorist attacks against our nation has been, "Why do they hate us?"—the "they" in this question ostensibly referring to the world's Arabs and Muslims. Many in our country, among them American Muslims, initially were reluctant to answer this question. This reluctance was born of a fear of being labeled unpatriotic, un-American—or worse, apologists for terrorists—by some of the ubiquitous commentators and talking heads who vociferously attacked anyone who dared pose this question in the immediate aftermath of the attacks.

Now, several months later [in March 2002], I think that this question finally should be addressed. Yet still, I hesitate. Not because I think the question is invalid, but rather because of the atmosphere of intellectual suffocation that remains prevalent in our nation—an atmosphere which has stifled reasoned discourse on this topic. And I hesitate because of concern that my loyalty, and that of our nation's seven million American Muslims, yet again will be questioned. This despite the fact that every major American Muslim organization and leader has condemned the horrible events of Sept. 11 and those responsible for them. We have repeatedly and unequivocally stated that there is no possible justification (religious or otherwise) for these acts on the basis [of] our faith, and that those who claim to commit such acts in the name of Islam have heinously twisted its teachings. And yet if we dare to explore the roots of this evil, our loyalties become immediately suspect in the eyes of some cynical pundits searching for an excuse to brand all Muslims—and indeed Islam itself—as civilization's new enemy.

THE TOP TEN COUNTRIES WITH THE LARGEST MUSLIM POPULATIONS

Taken from: "The Muslim World," Beyond the Wall, 2007, btw.imb.org.

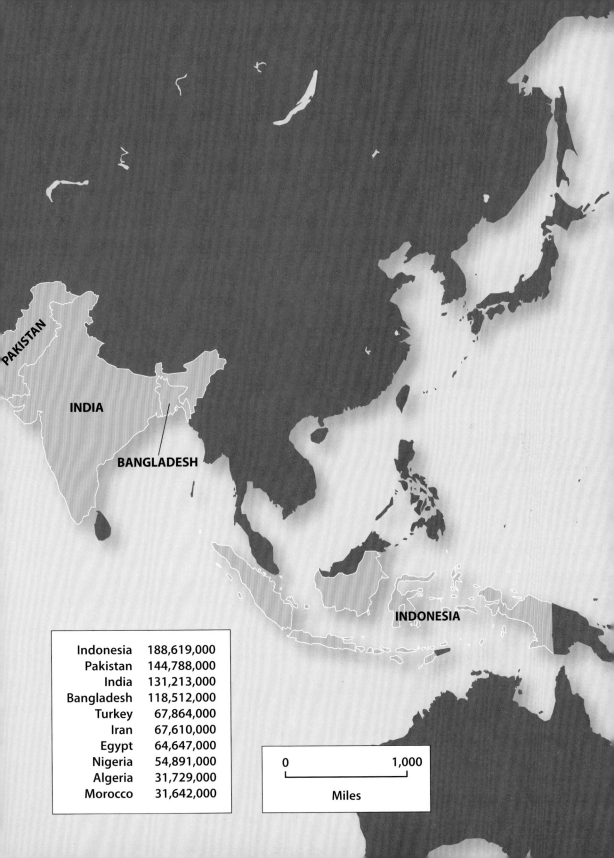

PAKISTAN

INDIA

BANGLADESH

INDONESIA

Indonesia	188,619,000
Pakistan	144,788,000
India	131,213,000
Bangladesh	118,512,000
Turkey	67,864,000
Iran	67,610,000
Egypt	64,647,000
Nigeria	54,891,000
Algeria	31,729,000
Morocco	31,642,000

0   1,000

Miles

A Misleading Generalization

In trying to characterize the motives of those suspected of perpetrating the terrorist attacks, President George W. Bush proclaimed that "they hate our way of life." This is at best a gross oversimplification, and at worst dangerously naive. Such jargon may sound nice for an 11 o'clock news sound bite, but it does not accurately answer the question, "Why do they hate us?"

Indeed, I would argue that the question itself is a misleading generalization, based on the erroneous assumption that Muslims and Arabs "hate us." The vast majority of Muslims and Arabs do not hate America, per se. Any statement to the contrary is a myth which only serves to perpetuate the dangerous, false "Islam-as-the-enemy" doctrine promoted by some self-styled experts on Islam. In fact, a great many Muslims and Arabs would cherish the opportunity to immigrate to the United States and enjoy the political, religious, economic, and educational freedoms that many of us take for granted. Those of us American Muslims and Arab-Americans who are either immigrants or the children of immigrants from the Muslim world are an undeniable testimony to this critical concept. Immigrants to the U.S. from the Arab and Muslim worlds and their descendants have been successful, educated, productive members of our society. In fact, we are the objects of envy among our friends and relatives overseas, who long to trace the footsteps of our parents or grandparents to this great land.

> Many [Muslims] express displeasure with the excesses of our overly materialistic culture, with a presumed emphasis on money, sex, and entertainment.

American Excess

Of course, this does not mean that there are not some aspects of our society that are frowned upon by the generally conservative communities of the Muslim world.

Many express displeasure with the excesses of our overly materialistic culture, with a presumed emphasis on money, sex, and entertainment. While this may definitely be a stereotypical perception on their part, we must bear in mind that this is the image of America promoted by Hollywood and the music industry. It is these elements of American society—as represented in movies, television soaps, and the latest music videos—to which individuals in the Muslim world are the most directly exposed and from which they derive their basic assumptions about our country. In this regard, certainly, Arabs and Muslims are not alone in their criticisms of our perceived decadent society. Similar complaints have

> Most Muslims and Arabs know that, like any other society or culture, America has its strengths and faults.

Some Muslim communities decry the U.S. culture of excess, as embodied by celebrity entertainers. (Ethan Miller/Getty Images for BASE Entertainment.)

been heard from all corners of the world—and indeed from within our own nation as well.

Of course, there are fringe elements in all societies who do not see shades of gray, but rather only the stark contrast of black and white, good and bad. These elements are prone to rejecting everything American as being inherently corrupt and a danger to their way of life. In a way, these individuals—who clearly represent a minority—are the counterparts of those extremists in our country who today clamor that Islam itself poses a clear and present danger to our country. Ironic, isn't it?

> Muslim and Arab resentment grows exponentially when they look toward . . . foreign policy stands of our country that are perceived as anti-Muslim and anti-Arab.

That said, most Muslims are sophisticated enough that they "don't throw the baby out with the bath water." Most Muslims and Arabs know that, like any other society or culture, America has its strengths and faults—and they hope to emulate these strengths in their own societies while avoiding those elements they find distasteful.

Muslim and Arab Resentment

Muslim and Arab resentment grows exponentially when they look toward other foreign policy stands of our country that are perceived as anti-Muslim and anti-Arab. Chief among these issues: the seemingly blind, unconditional support provided by the U.S. to Israel's brutal military occupation of Palestinian lands, expansionist settlement policy, and flagrant violation of innumerable international resolutions dealing with Palestinian political and human rights. Daily on the free-spirited Qatari satellite station, Al-Jazeera, they view images of American Apache helicopter gunships and U.S.-provided tanks, fighter jets, and missiles wreaking mayhem, destruction, and death on Palestinian towns and refugee camps. And they hear the somber pronouncements of various

American officials condemning "Palestinian terrorism" while failing even to acknowledge Palestinian suffering.

Arabs and Muslims also resent our country's decade-long sanctions policy against Iraq, which has resulted in the deaths of hundreds of thousands of Iraqi children from starvation and disease but left the brutal Iraqi dictator Saddam Hussein[1] more entrenched in power than ever. Why, they ask, do the innocent and noble Iraqi people have to suffer for the sins of their leader—a leader they did not choose and who for so long was supported by America?

Within this contextual framework, too, it is possible to comprehend the paradox of how Bin Laden's recent rantings against both America and Arab/Muslim regimes could gain widespread resonance with many Muslims who simultaneously and overwhelmingly condemned the barbaric atrocities of Sept. 11. Indeed, Bin Laden may be captured or killed by the time this is published.[2] As long as the fertile breeding ground of discontent and resentment persists, however, more Bin Ladens will emerge to fill the vacuum. And their message, too, will resonate with a disaffected and disenfranchised Muslim world. For Muslims, ironically, will be continuing to ask the same question: "Why do they hate us?"

Notes

1. The United States invaded Iraq in March 2003 and unseated Saddam Hussein, who was later executed for his crimes.
2. As of April 2010, Bin Laden has not been captured or killed.

Globalization Did Not Lead to the Attacks of 9/11

Brink Lindsey

Brink Lindsey, a scholar at the Cato Institute, a libertarian think tank, disputes the claim that globalization is to blame for the 9/11 attacks. In the following viewpoint, he asserts that globalization has not reached much of the Muslim world from which the 9/11 terrorists came. For example, Lindsey claims, few of the nations with ties to Islamist terrorism belong to the World Trade Organization. In fact, most Muslim nations do not trade freely with the rest of the world, nor do they take advantage of free-market policies that stimulate economic growth, he argues. While globalization can indeed bring turmoil to some developing nations, it also brings the hope that is lacking in many Muslim nations, Lindsey writes.

SOURCE. Brink Lindsey, "Poor Choice: Why Globalization Didn't Create 9/11," *The New Republic Online*, November 12, 2001. Reproduced by permission of *The New Republic*.

It's not surprising that the loony left blames globalization for the September 11 attacks. But what's David Held's excuse? Held is a prominent and respected globalization theorist who teaches at the prominent and respected London School of Economics. Yet in a recent [November 2001] article published in the online magazine *openDemocracy*, he opined, "In our global age shaped by the flickering images of television and new information systems, the gross inequalities of life chances found in many of the world's regions feed a frenzy of anger, hostility and resentment . . . [W]ithout an attempt to anchor globalisation in meaningful principles of social justice, there can be no durable solution to the kind of crimes we have just seen." And then there's Robert Kaiser, an associate editor of the *Washington Post*. "In the global village," he wrote in September [2001], "the poor know how poor they are, and how much better the rich are living. The resourceful poor won't accept their status passively, but try to change it. Millions of them have pursued that goal by sneaking into the United States, just as the perpetrators of [the 9/11] attacks did. They of course belong to a different category: the aggrieved who refuse to swallow their grievances."

The Economic Argument

Here, then, is the nonhysterical argument for globalization's culpability. The worldwide spread of market forces has created both winners and losers—not just within countries, but among them as well. The Muslim world is home to many of the losers. And, adding insult to injury, world-shrinking communications technology ensures that those on the bottom are constantly bombarded with images of those on top. No wonder they hate us.

It's true, of course, that many countries in the Muslim world are economic disasters. According to statistics compiled by economic historian Angus Maddison for the Organisation for Economic Co-operation and

Development [OECD], between 1985 and 1998, average per capita income declined in real terms in Iran, Iraq, Jordan, Qatar, Saudi Arabia, Syria, the United Arab Emirates, and Yemen. By contrast, it rose 30 percent in Israel, 50 percent in Uruguay, 90 percent in Chile, and more than doubled in China, Thailand, and South Korea. Such absolute and relative decline surely feeds feelings of inadequacy and hopelessness, thus heightening fanaticism's appeal.

The Problem with Blaming Globalization

But where the argument falls apart is in blaming globalization for Muslim countries' economic woes. For the sad fact is that, while newly liberated market forces have indeed fomented dramatic changes around the planet (mostly for the better), one place they haven't fomented dramatic—or even substantial—change is in the Islamic world. With a few notable exceptions—Turkey, Malaysia, Indonesia, some of the Gulf states—most Muslim countries have kept international economic integration at bay. Highly restrictive barriers to trade and investment choke off the international flows of goods, services, and capital. Nor has globalization reordered these countries internally. Pervasive economic controls stifle competition, while the institutional infrastructure on which markets depend remains pathetically underdeveloped. Most Muslim countries are more or less immune from globalization's creative destruction. They live in self-imposed exile from the new global economy. In other words, it is not globalization that fuels Al Qaeda—but its opposite. For if the challenges of adapting to global economic integration are daunting, they pale in comparison to the frustrations of living in the defunct and discredited collectivist past.

> "It is not globalization that fuels Al Qaeda—but its opposite."

Afghanistan, Algeria, Iran, Iraq, Libya, Saudi Arabia, Sudan, Syria, and Yemen—all are under the microscope these days for their ties to Islamist terrorism. Guess what else they have in common? None belongs to the World Trade Organization—which, with 142 members, is hardly an exclusive club. And that's just one symptom of their economic disengagement. The Fraser Institute's Economic Freedom of the World report (co-published by my employer, the Cato Institute) rates more than 100 countries based on the openness of their trade and investment policies. According to the "trade openness index" featured in the 2001 report, Pakistan, Bangladesh, Syria, Algeria, and Iran all rank in the bottom quintile of countries surveyed. Not a single Arab or South Asian country makes the top half of the list. (Oman, at 59 out of 109 countries, ranks highest in the region.) Afghanistan, Iraq, Libya, Saudi Arabia, Sudan, and Yemen aren't even included in the report because of a lack of reliable data.

Mike Moore, director general of the World Trade Organization (WTO), speaks in Geneva in 2001. Many nations that Islamist terrorists come from do not participate in international organizations such as the WTO. (**AP Images.**)

While oil does provide an economic link between some Middle Eastern countries and the outside world, most other forms of transnational commerce barely exist. In Egypt and Sudan, exports equal around 2 percent of gross domestic product [GDP]; in Pakistan and Bangladesh, it's roughly 3 percent. By comparison, in emerging markets Mexico and Thailand, exports exceed 15 percent of GDP. Nor are most Muslim countries attracting foreign investment. As of 1998, just 2 percent of American direct investment occurred in Africa and the Middle East, according to the OECD. The numbers are similar for the UK, Japan, France, and Germany.

QUALITY OF LIFE IN THE MUSLIM WORLD IN 2000

Country	Population (million)	% Using the Internet	Gross Domestic Product per person/family
Afghanistan	26.8	0	$800
Algeria	31.7	.1	$5,500
Egypt	69.5	.3	$3,600
Indonesia	228.4	Data not available	$2,900
Iran	66.1	.2	$6,300
Iraq	23.3	Data not available	$2,500
Libya	5.2	0	$8,900
Pakistan	144.6	0	$2,000
Saudi Arabia	22.8	1.4	$10,500
Syria	16.7	0	$3,100

Taken from: M.H. Cooper, "Key Players in the Islamic World," *CQ Researcher*, November 23, 2001.

Insulated from Economic Liberty

Of course, globalization is about more than simply trade and investment. It also means domestic economic liberalization—the worldwide move from state-dominated models of economic development to more market-oriented policies—that is, macroeconomic stabilization, privatization of state-owned industries, elimination of price and entry controls, and reform of legal institutions. And, on this score too, most Muslim countries have insulated themselves. Since independence, collectivism of one stripe or another has dominated economic policymaking in the Islamic world. In Egypt, Syria, Iraq, and Libya, "Arab socialism" in various permutations was the guiding ideology; in Iran, Shah Mohammad Reza Pahlavi's White Revolution was followed by the ayatollahs' Islamic Revolution, and in the process government controls over economic life grew from extensive to sweeping.

> Globalization is a messy, disruptive process, but it can't explain Islamist extremism because it hasn't touched most of the Islamic world.

While the past decade has witnessed tentative moves by some countries—Egypt, for instance—toward economic reform, the collectivist legacy remains largely intact.

Consider two basic indicators of state involvement in the domestic economy: the relative importance of state-owned enterprises and the extent of price controls. The Economic Freedom of the World report rates countries on a scale from 0 to 10 with respect to both criteria: Scores of 6, 8, and 10 indicate increasingly market-oriented environments, while scores of 4, 2, and 0 identify progressively greater government ownership and control. Out of 13 surveyed countries—Algeria, Bahrain, Bangladesh, Egypt, Iran, Jordan, Kuwait, Morocco, Oman, Pakistan, Syria, Tunisia, and the United Arab Emirates [UAE]—only one, the UAE, earned solidly promarket scores (6 on state-owned enterprises, 8 on price controls). Over 80 percent of the scores were 4 and below.

Globalization is a messy, disruptive process, but it can't explain Islamist extremism because it hasn't touched most of the Islamic world. Indeed, that's a big part of the problem. Expanding markets may bring turmoil, but they also bring opportunity and hope—qualities in decidedly short supply in many Muslim countries. The once bright and exhilarating promises of centrally planned modernization have all long since faded, and no new vision of progress has yet taken hold. In that bleak twilight of despair, the temptation to reject modernity altogether grows ever more alluring.

Although Anti-Terrorism Strategies Have Made the United States Safer, Vigilance Is Necessary

Melvin A. Goodman

In the following viewpoint, national security scholar Melvin A. Goodman argues that many of the strategies implemented in response to the 9/11 attacks have made the United States safer. For example, he claims, the CIA has successfully disrupted al Qaeda and has limited Osama bin Laden's ability to operate. Moreover, Goodman maintains, the National Counterterrorism Center has established a central location for terrorism intelligence and has better connected the many intelligence agencies. However, continuing flaws in the CIA and mistakes made by the Department of Homeland Security demonstrate that much work remains. Terrorists continue to operate worldwide, Goodman asserts, which demands effective management of

SOURCE. Melvin A. Goodman, "America Is Safer Since 9/11," *Christian Science Monitor*, September 18, 2006. Reproduced by permission of the author.

intelligence funds. Goodman, an analyst for the CIA from 1966 to 1990, is a scholar at the Center for International Policy.

T he attacks on the World Trade Center and the Pentagon five years ago [September 11, 2001] exposed fundamental weaknesses in America's intelligence community, particularly the FBI and the CIA. The absence of any terrorist attacks against the United States since 9/11 suggests that the reorganizations and reforms of the past five years, as well as increased vigilance, have made the nation safer. The intelligence picture remains complicated, however, and much work needs to be done to limit our vulnerability to international terrorism.

Notable Achievements

There have been several notable achievements, starting with the operational success of the CIA against Al Qaeda since 2001. Too much attention has been devoted to the failure to capture Osama bin Laden, and not enough attention has been given to the logistical and financial disruption of his organization that has limited Mr. bin Laden's ability to plan follow-up operations in the United States and to operate abroad.

The CIA and the FBI, along with foreign intelligence liaison services, have operated effectively in capturing and killing top Al Qaeda leaders. But when FBI Director Robert Mueller III claimed to know that "Al Qaeda maintains the ability and the intent to inflict significant casualties in the US with little warning," the congressional intelligence committees should have demanded his evidence.

The creation of the National Counterterrorism Center in January 2005 has provided the beginning of a central repository for terrorism information and greater connectivity among all 16 intelligence agencies and

their databases. The CIA dominates the staffing of the counterterrorism center, but all agencies are represented, and these representatives are charged with sharing information with their sponsoring agencies. There has been greater consolidation of information, particularly a more comprehensive watch-listing system that could have prevented 9/11 terrorists Khalid al-Midhar and Nawaf al-Hazmi from falling through the cracks.

There is still an inadequate flow of information between federal and state or local intelligence agencies, and the military leadership of the National Counterterrorism Center seems ill-suited to nurture the strategic intelligence needed for a long-term campaign against terrorism.

The CIA has streamlined its own counterterrorism center, concentrating on more innovative operational plans. The center is better connected to other intelligence agencies, but it has not abandoned the "fusion center" concept that mixes intelligence analysts and clandestine operatives. The fusion of analysts and operatives has led to politicized intelligence, with the worst-case notions of agency operatives influencing the final intelligence product.

Work to Be Done

Much is left to be done. The 9/11 commission's recommendation of a director of national intelligence was a bad idea that has been made worse by bureaucratic growth. The office of the director has a budget of more than $1 billion and a staff of more than 1,000. Too many high-level staffers have been recruited from the CIA and other intelligence agencies, further weakening these agencies. And little has been done to limit the Pentagon's control over nearly 85 percent of the intelligence budget and 90 percent of intelligence personnel. The undersecretary of defense for intelligence, Stephen Cambone, has more influence over the day-to-day management of the com-

Photo on previous page: After the terrorist attacks on September 11, 2001, a restructuring of U.S. intelligence agencies sapped the CIA and other agencies of key personnel. (Saul Loeb/ AFP/Getty Images.)

> "The Department of Homeland Security's inept handling of hurricane Katrina and the FBI's feckless campaign against Arab and Muslim immigrants . . . demonstrate that much work needs to be done."

munity than the director of national intelligence, John Negroponte.

The CIA's fundamental flaws have gone largely uncorrected. Far too much attention is given to current and tactical intelligence and insufficient attention to the big-picture needs of strategic intelligence. The CIA worries about the intelligence needs of the warfighter and devotes too little to the long-term geopolitical interests of the policymaker. It is unlikely that the recent appointment of a four-star general, Michael Hayden, will correct this problem, and that Mr. Hayden was director of the National Security Agency and defended the policy of warrantless eavesdropping does not augur well for the credibility of the CIA.

The CIA's extralegal activities, particularly renditions and secret prisons, have complicated the task of maintaining credible relations with our allies in the battle against terrorism. An Italian court recently demanded the extradition of 24 CIA operatives, whose pathetic tradecraft left agency fingerprints over their rendition efforts.

Last, the Department of Homeland Security's inept handling of hurricane Katrina and the FBI's feckless campaign against Arab and Muslim immigrants in the United States demonstrate that much work needs to be done at both agencies. The nation lacks one central repository for all information on national and international terrorism; the Department of Homeland Security should be the home of this repository. The FBI still lacks an effective computer system to coordinate intelligence information, which is central to preventing another terrorist attack.

The greatest setback to US efforts has been the profligate military campaign in Iraq, which created a new source of terrorism and terrorists, thus weakening the campaign against terrorism and US national security. There were very few jihadists [those who participate in Islamic holy war] in Iraq before we invaded.

Overall, the post-9/11 changes have made us safer over the short term, but as long as terrorists can operate the world over, we must demand better management of our $45-billion intelligence and $40-billion homeland security industries.

Anti-Terrorism Laws Created in Response to 9/11 Compromise Civil Liberties Worldwide

Erika Waak

In the rush to strengthen national security following the attacks of 9/11, nations worldwide have implemented laws that threaten civil liberties, claims Erika Waak in the following viewpoint. Laws that increase the ease with which law enforcement can conduct surveillance, intercept communications, and search and seize personal property have increased significantly, she maintains. Increased access to personal information combined with improvements in technology have allowed governments to invade personal privacy with little oversight, Waak asserts. Even international organizations have called for increased sharing of personal information among nations, some of which have long-standing surveillance policies, she argues. Vigilance is

SOURCE. Erika Waak, "The Global Reach of Privacy Invasion," *The Humanist*, vol. 62, November-December 2002, pp. 62–68. Copyright © 2002 by the American Humanist Association. Reproduced by permission.

necessary to protect the right to privacy. Waak writes for *The Humanist*, a magazine that applies the philosophy of humanism, which affirms personal fulfillment and a responsibility to the greater good of humanity.

I n the aftermath of September 11, 2001, civil liberties have been compromised not only in the United States but in countries all over the world. New antiterrorism laws, particularly those which expand the surveillance authority of the state, now threaten political freedom on every continent. Furthermore, efforts to reverse this trend are complicated by the fact that most of what is going on is generally unknown to the citizens of each affected nation.

The Scope of the Problem

The full scope of this problem was brought to light on September 3, 2002, when the Electronic Privacy Information Center (EPIC), in association with Privacy International (PI), released the fifth annual privacy and human rights report. The study, entitled *Privacy and Human Rights: An International Survey of Privacy Laws and Developments*, reveals the current state of privacy in over fifty countries, including the United States. Marc Rotenberg, executive director of EPIC, links cause and effect in the foreword: "In the rush to strengthen national security and to reduce the risk of future terrorist acts, governments around the world turned to legal authority and new technology to extend control over individuals." And they did so without adequately considering the long-term impact on democratic freedoms.

However, the panic hasn't been limited to individual nations alone. International bodies have gotten into the act—and indeed have been among the first to do so. The United Nations took immediate action right after the attacks and adopted on September 12, 2001, UN

Resolution 1368 that calls for increased cooperation between countries to suppress and prevent terrorism. The Committee of Ministers of the Council of Europe issued a similar declaration, and the North Atlantic Treaty Organization [NATO] reasserted its own Article 5, which declares that an attack on any NATO nation constitutes an attack on all.

Then on September 26, 2001, the Parliamentary Assembly of the Council of Europe called for the ratification by individual countries of existing antiterrorist conventions. This included the lifting of caveats in these agreements and the extension of police activity to cover "terrorist messages and the decoding thereof." The European Union, in a report on October 17, 2001, proposed a common European arrest warrant, a common framework for antiterrorist laws, increased international cooperation among police and intelligence authorities, and a greater capability for freezing assets and preventing money laundering. Along these latter lines, the Organization for Economic Co-operation and Development together with the G-7, consisting of the world's seven largest industrial market economies, and European Commission called for an extension of its mandate to act against terrorist financing. Looking at the Internet, the European Commission went so far as to consider a requirement that every European Union member nation pass laws making cyber attacks a terrorist offense.

> "Wiretapping abuses have even occurred in the most democratic countries, such as Denmark and Sweden."

Early Developments

All of these calls by international bodies for increased cooperation and stiffer laws gave various governments the momentum to quickly develop new antiterrorist legislation. The Privacy and Human Rights report chronicles the early developments:

New Zealand minimized public consultation on a proposed law to freeze the financial assets of suspected terrorists because the government felt it was bound by United Nations Security Council resolutions. France expanded police powers to search private property without warrants. Germany reduced authorization restraints on interception of communications and increased data sharing between law enforcement and national security agencies.

Australia and Canada both introduced laws to redefine *terrorist activity* and to grant powers of [domestic] surveillance to national security agencies. . . . India passed a law to allow authorities to detain suspects without trial, conduct increased wiretapping, and seize funds and property. The United Kingdom passed a law permitting the retention of data for law enforcement purposes in contravention to existing data protection rules. The United States passed a number of laws, including the USA-PATRIOT Act, which increases surveillance powers and minimizes oversight and due process requirements.

The report sums up events of the past year [2002] by noting that "almost every country that changed its laws to reflect the environment following September 11 increased the ability of law enforcement and national security agencies to perform interception of communications, and transformed the powers of search and seizure, and an increase in the type of data that can be accessed."

Longstanding Surveillance Programs

Unfortunately, the recent and widespread loss of liberty is only part of the story. These new intrusions by governments into the lives of citizens merely add to an environment already saturated with longstanding programs of surveillance. Since these programs aren't widely known, a general summary is in order.

In most countries, national governments issue citizen and resident identity cards that not only make invasive profiling possible but also easily enable profiles to be reproduced when the cards are misplaced. At one point a plan was underway in the United States to make state driver's licenses part of a sophisticated, nationwide ID system. A broad coalition of civil liberties groups, however, has so far managed to stall this proposal.

New Technologies

With the continuous evolution of cheaper and more sophisticated technologies, governments have been able to increase their deployment of audio bugging devices. Some of them can now be as tiny as an office staple. And for the last fifteen years, the U.S. government has led a global effort to boost the capability of intelligence agencies to eavesdrop on personal conversations. Meanwhile, video surveillance cameras that monitor private and public places throughout the world are ubiquitous while, out of sight, satellite surveillance cameras spy from high above the Earth using lenses capable of detecting objects less than one meter square anywhere on the planet.

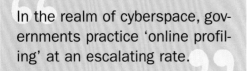

In the realm of cyberspace, governments practice 'online profiling' at an escalating rate.

Wiretaps are widely used—sometimes in individual countries on such a vast scale that they involve thousands of connections that operate effortlessly. Targeted individuals are typically human rights workers, political opponents, and student activists. Wiretapping abuses have even occurred in the most democratic countries, such as Denmark and Sweden, where intelligence agencies conducted surveillance of thousands of leftists for nearly forty years.

In order to more easily conduct wiretaps, government agencies now establish formulated arrangements with

A.U.B. armen houden zoals afgebeeld.

3 sec.

Please, raise arms according to picture.

telecommunications providers so that phone systems are made "wiretap friendly" in ways unknown to the public. In this regard, the U.S. Congress approved in 1994 the Communications Assistance for Law Enforcement Act, which outlines the legal requirement that all telephone systems provide surveillance capabilities. The act supports the government's two primary strategies: to promote mandatory laws requiring all companies that develop phones and communications technologies to build in surveillance capabilities and to limit the development and distribution of products that provide encryptions which scramble communications and files so others can't read them.

Many governments also use biometrics, which attempt to verify an individual's identity based on physiological or behavioral characteristics and compare new samples of that person's characteristics with those previously

Body scanners let airport authorities see through passengers' clothing. (**AP Images.**)

captured. The most common biometric methods are fingerprinting, DNA identification, and voice recognition. The latest development in biometric technology is the automation of the verification process by converting each sample into an algorithm which is used for matching purposes. Daily movements and habits of a person can then be tracked by creating an electronic trail of that person's actions.

Invasion of Cyberspace

In the realm of cyberspace, governments practice "online profiling" at an escalating rate. This practice involves tracking an individual's Internet activity in ways that can reveal financial, medical, and other private information in only a few minutes while the individual being tracked visits dozens of websites. This practice is analogous to a government spy following a given person through a shopping mall, monitoring everything the person looks at and purchases. Also, corporations share personal information with governments by using computer logs to capture consumer information.

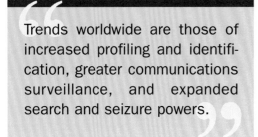

Trends worldwide are those of increased profiling and identification, greater communications surveillance, and expanded search and seizure powers.

Governments also work through Internet service providers to place "black boxes" on their networks. These monitor user traffic without public knowledge, presumably for security and maintenance purposes, and are linked to government agencies by high-speed connections. The Council of Europe acknowledges this privacy problem in its *Explanatory Report of the Convention on Cybercrime*, released on November 8, 2001, that says:

> The collection of this data may, in some situations, permit the compilation of a profile of a person's interests, associates and social context. Accordingly Parties should

bear such considerations in mind when establishing the appropriate safeguards and legal prerequisites for undertaking such measures.

Heavy lobbying by civil liberties activists exempted U.S. Internet Service Providers (ISPs) from adhering to technical requirements that intercept communications. By contrast, in Australia the Telecommunications Act of 1997 obligates telecommunications operators to assist law enforcement at their own cost. A telecommunications act in the Netherlands, approved in 1998, requires ISPs receiving a court order to intercept all traffic and maintain user logs for three months.

There are two international bodies leading the way in increased surveillance of all communication and activities of Internet users: the Council of Europe and the G-8, including Canada, France, Germany, Italy, Japan, Russia, the United Kingdom, and the United States. The Council of Europe formed a Committee of Experts on Crime in Cyberspace (PC-CY) and created the Draft Convention on Cyber-crime, version 27, released in April 2000, that significantly promotes surveillance. Also, in May 2002 the European Parliament reversed its 1997 Telecommunications Privacy Directive and allowed each European Union government to enact laws to maintain the location and traffic data of all users of mobile and landline phones, e-mails, the Internet, and more.

International Data Sharing

Meanwhile, governments are, without specific judicial authorization, changing the application of legislation from national security to criminal investigation and prevention, and many governments are increasingly sharing data with each other. As a result, information originally collected for one purpose gets used for another. The goal of these governments is to create profiles of many individuals, mostly travelers, whether or not they are citizens of a given country.

Along these lines, the U.S. National Security Agency operates an international intelligence and law enforcement surveillance system known as Echelon. This is done in cooperation with Australia, Canada, New Zealand, and the United Kingdom. Echelon has existed since the beginning of the Cold War and, today, is an electronic surveillance network that can intercept most of the world's telephone calls, faxes, and e-mails, and shares this information with the five-member intelligence alliance.

The largest U.S. domestic surveillance system is described in a September 4, 2002, *Washington Post* article on airline security. It says the Transportation Security Administration (TSA) is developing a secret profiling system known as the second-generation Computer Assisted Passenger Prescreening System (CAPPS II). This profiling system is a vast network of supercomputers that gathers personal data on everyone so that, when a person books a flight, her or his background is checked for clues about possible plans of violence.

TSA has not resolved issues concerning the impact that CAPPS II will have on civil liberties. Civil liberties activists warn that privacy issues could create controversy if these concerns are not publicly resolved before the system begins operation. They are worried that innocent individuals who are offbeat or politically radical will be singled out by the system which challenges the right to privacy, the right to travel, and the right to engage in certain activities.

Clearly, the major relevant trends worldwide are those of increased profiling and identification, greater communications surveillance, and expanded search and seizure powers. In connection with this, we find a decrease in data protection regimes and an increase in data sharing, particularly with governments. These activities tend to quickly become codified into law. And the process has accelerated in response to the events of 9-11 with many legislative shifts occurring worldwide that affected the four primary areas of privacy: information privacy, bodily privacy, privacy of communication, and territorial privacy.

Protecting Privacy

Fortunately, the right of privacy is included in the constitution of nearly every country in the world. Often, when it is not included, ordinary laws and provisions cover the matter. *The Privacy and Human Rights* report defines privacy as "a way of drawing the line at how far society can intrude into a person's affairs." U.S. Supreme Court Justice Louis Brandeis said in the 1890s that privacy should be reflected in the U.S. Constitution and argued that an individual's right to privacy is the most cherished freedom in a democracy. The preamble to the Australian Privacy Charter is in agreement, saying:

> A free and democratic society requires respect for the autonomy of individuals, and limits on the power of both state and private organizations to intrude on that autonomy. . . . Privacy is a key value that underpins human dignity and other key values such as freedom of association and freedom of speech. . . . Privacy is a basic human right and the reasonable expectation of every person.

The UN commissioner on human rights in 1988 declared:

> Compliance with Article 17 requires that the integrity and confidentiality of correspondence should be guaranteed de jure and de facto. Correspondence should be delivered to the addressee without interception and without being opened or otherwise read. Surveillance,

whether electronic or otherwise, interceptions of telephonic, telegraphic and other forms of communication, wire-tapping and recording of conversations should be prohibited.

Countries in Europe, Asia, and Latin America continue to enforce data protection laws. The new European Union Electronic Communication Directive prohibits unsolicited commercial marketing by e-mail without consent and protects mobile phone users from surveillance. Bulgaria endorsed in January 2002 its new Personal Data Protection Act. Poland approved in May 2002 the Convention for the Protection of Individuals with Regard to Automatic Processing of Personal Data. Slovenia amended its Data Protection Act in 2001 to establish an independent supervisory authority. Malaysia's Personal Data Protection Act is pending, and a National Internet Advisory Committee in Singapore released a Model Data Protection Code for the Private Sector in February 2002. Peru enacted a data protection law in August 2001 covering credit-reporting agencies, and both Peru and Mexico passed new freedom of information laws in 2002. A similar law also went into effect in Poland.

> Constant vigilance and activism on the part of people all over the world remain necessary to ensure that privacy rights prevail in this new century.

Governments are also responding to the right to privacy in the workplace. Finland adopted a new law on Data Protection in Working Life in October 2001 and the president of the Russian Federation signed a new labor code that includes the security of personal data. The United Kingdom privacy commissioner drafted a four-part code on data protection in the workplace, and in March 2002 a national committee in Sweden issued a proposal recommending specific legislation to protect the personal information of employees in both the private and public sectors. The European Union's Data Protection Working Party released in May 2002 a working paper about the monitoring of electronic communication in the workplace. The Hong Kong Data Protection Commission issued for public consultation in June 2002 a draft code of practice in the workplace.

Clearly then, there are a number of new provisions that ensure the protection of privacy. This provides a glimmer of hope in a world where many new anti-terrorism and security measures work against human rights to increase communications surveillance, to profile individuals, and to weaken data protection regimes. But constant vigilance and activism on the part of people all over the world remain necessary to ensure that privacy rights prevail in this new century.

Racial Profiling Is Necessary in the Wake of 9/11

Peter H. Schuck

In light of the tragic terrorist attacks of September 11, 2001, law enforcement officials should be able to use profiling techniques to protect Americans, argues Yale Law School professor Peter H. Schuck. In the viewpoint that follows, he explains that when faced with competing risks—the time-consuming process of interviewing all passengers boarding an airplane, for example, or the potential tragedy of random interviews that fail to identify a terrorist—profiling makes sense. Indeed, he claims, while all stereotypes are too broad, they are often true. Gender, size, body type, and dress, Schuck suggests, offer law enforcement reasonable clues about whom to screen for questioning. However, he reasons, such stereotypes are no longer useful at later stages of the legal process, when such stereotypes deny equality in the eyes of the law. Schuck is author of *The Limits of Law: Essays on Democratic Governance*.

SOURCE. Peter H. Schuck, "A Case for Profiling: There's a Reason We Use Stereotypes. They Work: The Challenge Is How to Use Them Selectively and Administer Them Wisely," *American Lawyer*, vol. 24, January 2002, pp. 59–61. Reproduced by permission of the author.

Racial profiling has become the hottest civil rights issue of the day, but it deserves cooler reflection than it has received. Politicians and pundits, regardless of their politics, reflexively denounce it; nary a word is raised in its defense. Many states have already barred it, and Congress is likely to do so.[1] Some police chiefs resist Justice Department interrogation policies they think entail profiling. Yet September 11, [2001] as Dr. [Samuel] Johnson[2] said of the gallows, concentrates the mind wonderfully. The disaster that befell us then—and might recur in some form—necessitates a profiling debate that is clear-eyed and hardheaded, not demagogic.

The furor about racial profiling is easy to understand. "Driving while black" and "flying while Arab" are emblems of the indignities that law enforcement officials are said to inflict on minorities on the basis of demeaning stereotypes and racial prejudice. This is no laughing matter. Respect for the rule of law means that people must not be singled out for enforcement scrutiny simply because of their race or ethnicity.

Or does it? Much turns on the meaning of "simply" in the last sentence. Profiling is not only inevitable but sensible public policy, under certain conditions and with appropriate safeguards against abuse. After September 11, the stakes in deciding when and how profiling may be used and how to remedy abuses when they occur could not be higher.

Examining Our Values

A fruitful debate on profiling properly begins with our values as a society. The most important of these, of course, is self-defense, without which no other values can be realized. But we should be wary of claims that we must sacrifice our ideals in the name of national security; this means that other ideals remain central to the inquiry. The one most threatened by profiling is the principle that all individuals are equal before the law by reason of their membership in a political community committed to formal equality. In most but not all respects, we extend the same entitlement to aliens who are present in the polity legally or illegally. Differential treatment must meet a burden of justification—in the case of racial classifications, a very high one.

This ideal has a corollary: Government may not treat individuals arbitrarily. To put this principle another way, it must base its action on information that is reliable enough to justify its exercise of power over free individuals. How good must the information be? The law's answer is that it depends. Criminal punishment requires proof beyond a reasonable doubt, while a tort judgment demands only the preponderance of the evidence. Health agencies can often act with little more than a rational suspicion that a substance might be dangerous. A consular official can deny a visa if in her "opinion" the applicant is likely to become a public charge and unlike the previous examples, courts may not review this decision. Information good enough for one kind of decision, then, is not nearly good enough for others. Context is everything.

Competing Risks

This brings us to profiling by law enforcement officials. Consider the context in which an FBI agent must search for the September 11 terrorists, or a security officer at a railroad and airline terminal must screen for new ones. Vast numbers of individuals pass through the officer's line of vision, and they do so only fleetingly, for a few seconds at most. As a result, the official must make a decision about each of them within those few seconds, unless she is prepared to hold all of them up for the time it will take to interrogate each, one by one. She knows absolutely nothing about these individuals, other than the physical characteristics that she can immediately observe, and learning more about them through inter-rogation will take a lot of time. The time this would take is costly to her task; each question she stops to ask will either allow others to pass by unnoticed or prolong the wait of those in the already long, steadily lengthening line. The time is even more costly to those waiting in line; for them, more than for her, time is money and opportunity. Politicians know how their constituents hate lines and constantly press her—along with customs, immigration, and toll officials—to shorten them.

> Although all stereotypes are overbroad, most are probably correct much more often than they are wrong; that is why they are useful.

At the same time, her risks of being wrong are dra-matically asymmetrical. If she stops everyone, she will cause all of the problems just described and all of the people (except one, perhaps) will turn out to be perfectly innocent. On the other hand, if she fails to stop the one person among them who is in fact a terrorist, she causes a social calamity of incalculable proportions. In choos-ing, as she must, between these competing risks, her self-interest and the social interest will drive her in the direction of avoiding calamity. The fact that society also tells her to be evenhanded only adds to her dilemma, while providing no useful guidance as to what to do, given these incentives.

So what should she do? We can get at this question by asking what we would do were we in her place. To answer this question, we need not engage in moral speculation but can look to our own daily experiences. Each day, we all face choices that are very similar in structure, albeit far less consequential. We must make decisions very rapidly about things that matter to us. We know that our information is inadequate to the choice, but we also know that we cannot in the time available get informa-tion that is sufficiently better to improve our decision significantly. We consider our risks of error, which are often asymmetrical. Because we must momentarily integrate all this uncertainty into a concrete choice, we resort to shortcuts to decisionmaking. (Psychologists call these "heuristics.")

The Advantages and Disadvantages of Stereotypes

The most important and universal of these tactical shortcuts is the stereotype. The advantage of stereotypes is that they economize on information, enabling us to choose quickly when our information is inadequate. This is a great, indeed indispensable virtue, precisely because this problem is ubiquitous in daily life—so ubiquitous that we scarcely notice it; nor do we notice how often we use stereotypes to solve it. Indeed, we could not live without stereotypes. We use them in order to predict how others will behave, as when we assume that blacks will vote Democratic (though many do not) and to anticipate others' desires, needs, or expectations, as when we offer help to disabled people (though some of them find this presumptuous). We use them when we take safety precautions when a large, unkempt, angry-looking man approaches us on a dark street (though he may simply be asking directions), and when we assume that higher-status schools are better (though they often prove to be unsuitable). Such assumptions are especially important in a mass society where people know less and less about one another.

Stereotypes, of course, have an obvious downside: They are sometimes wrong, almost by definition. After all, if they were wrong all the time, no rational person would use them, and if they were never wrong, they would be indisputable facts, not stereotypes. Stereotypes fall somewhere in between these extremes, but it is hard to know precisely where, because we seldom know precisely how accurate they are. Although all stereotypes are

overbroad, most are probably correct much more often than they are wrong; that is why they are useful. But when a stereotype is wrong, those who are exceptions to it naturally feel that they have not been treated equally as individuals, and they are right. Their uniqueness is being overlooked so that others can use stereotypes for the much larger universe of cases where the stereotypes are true and valuable. In this way, the palpable claims of discrete individuals are sacrificed to a disembodied social interest. This sacrifice offends not just them but others among us who identify with their sense of injustice, and when their indignation is compounded by the discourtesy or bias of bag checkers or law enforcement agents, the wound is even more deeply felt.

This is where the law comes in. When we view these stereotype-based injustices as sufficiently grave, we prohibit them. Even then, however, we do so only in a qualified way that expresses our ambivalence. Civil rights law,

Reliance on stereotypes impedes the justice system but can enhance security measures. (**Chris Hondros/ Getty Images.**)

for example, proscribes racial, gender, disability, and age stereotyping. At the same time, it allows government, employers, and others to adduce a public interest or business reason strong enough to justify using them. The law allows religious groups to hire only coreligionists. Officials drawing legislative districts may to some extent treat all members of a minority group as if they all had the same political interests. The military can bar women from certain combat roles. Employers can assume that women are usually less suitable for jobs requiring very heavy lifting. Such practices reflect stereotypes that are thought to be reasonable in general, though false as to particular individuals.

> No one would think it unjust for [an] officer to screen for Osama bin Laden, who is a very tall man with a beard and turban, by stopping all men meeting that general description.

The Importance of Context

Can the same be said of racial or ethnic profiling? Again, context is everything. We would object to a public college that categorically admitted women rather than men on the theory that women tend to be better students not because the stereotype is false, but because the school can readily ascertain academic promise on an individualized basis when reviewing applicants' files, which it must do anyway. On the other hand, no one would think it unjust for our officer to screen for Osama bin Laden, who is a very tall man with a beard and turban, by stopping all men meeting that general description. This is so not only because the stakes in apprehending him are immense, but also because in making instantaneous decisions about whom to stop, the official can use gender, size, physiognomy, and dress as valuable clues. She would be irresponsible and incompetent not to do so even though every man she stopped was likely to be a false positive and thus to feel unjustly treated for having been singled out.

Racial profiling in more typical law enforcement set-tings can raise difficult moral questions. Suppose that society views drug dealing as a serious vice, and that a disproportionate number of drug dealers are black men, although of course many are not. Would this stereotype justify stopping black men simply because of their color? Clearly not. The law properly requires more particular-ized evidence of wrongdoing. Suppose further, however, that police were to observe a black man engaging in the ostensibly furtive behavior that characterizes most but not all drug dealers, behavior also engaged in by some innocent men. Here, the behavioral stereotype would legally justify stopping the man. But what if the officer relied on both stereotypes in some impossible-to-parse combination? What if the behavioral stereotype alone had produced a very close call, and the racial one pushed it over the line?

Creating a Sensible Profiling Policy

Although I cannot answer all these questions, most critics of racial profiling do not even ask them. A wise policy will insist that the justice of profiling depends on a number of variables. How serious is the crime risk? How do we feel about the relative costs of false positives and false negatives? How accurate is the stereotype? How practicable is it to pursue the facts through an individualized inquiry rather than through stereotypes? If stereotypes must be used, are there some that rely on less incendiary and objectionable factors?

> It is now a cliché that September 11 changed our world. Profiling is bound to be part of the new dispensation.

A sensible profiling policy will also recognize that safeguards become more essential as the enforcement process progresses. Stereotypes that are reasonable at the stage of deciding whom to screen for questioning may be unacceptable at the later stages of arrest and prosecution, when official decisions should be based on more individualized information and when lawyers and other procedural safeguards can be made available. Screening officials can be taught about the many exceptions to even serviceable stereotypes, to recognize them when they appear, and to behave in ways that encourage those being screened not to take it personally.

It is now a cliché that September 11 changed our world. Profiling is bound to be part of the new dispensation. Clearer thinking and greater sensitivity to its potential uses and abuses can help produce both a safer and a more just America.

Notes

1. On June 17, 2003, the Justice Department issued guidelines that prohibit federal law enforcement agencies from racial profiling. End Racial Profiling Acts have been introduced by both houses in 2001, 2004, and 2007. None thus far have become law.
2. Johnson, an esteemed eighteenth-century author and philosopher, opposed capital punishment, at least for nonviolent crimes.

Racial Profiling Is Not Necessary in the Wake of 9/11

American Civil Liberties Union

In the following viewpoint, excerpted from the report *Sanctioned Bias: Racial Profiling Since 9/11*, the American Civil Liberties Union (ACLU) argues that even law enforcement veterans think that racial profiling—targeting people based on their national origin, ethnicity, or religion—is a lazy method of law enforcement. Because racial profiling casts such a wide net, the practice wastes time and resources, the ACLU claims. Moreover, racial profiling separates families, threatens businesses, and turns law enforcement against law-abiding immigrant citizens, therefore alienating communities that could provide much-needed intelligence. Not only is racial profiling un-American, the practice poses a national security risk by ignoring people who pose a threat but who do not meet the profile.

SOURCE. *Sanctioned Bias: Racial Profiling Since 9/11*. New York: ACLU, 2004. Copyright © 2004 ACLU, 125 Broad Street, 18th Floor, New York, NY 10004. Reproduced by permission.

Veterans of law enforcement who were police officers during the 1980s and 1990s, when the "war on drugs" was in full swing and racial profiling was rampant, are among the country's most knowledgeable experts on the effectiveness of racial profiling in fighting crime. Here are some of their comments:

Lazy Law Enforcement

Barbara A. Markham has been a police officer with the Oak Point Police Department in North Texas since 1983. She has been an undercover narcotics investigator since 1986, and is the recipient of awards and letters of commendation from the Department of Treasury—Bureau of Alcohol, Tobacco and Firearms for her investigative work. She has also been an outspoken critic of the Texas police for engaging in racial profiling in the enforcement of narcotics laws—profiling that has focused virtually exclusively on African Americans. In a recent interview, Officer Markham told the ACLU:

> Racial profiling is utilized when you have no intelligence and you're just casting a wide net and having to use a process of elimination out of that wide net. Racial profiling is a lazy method for law enforcement. You're not using investigative leads; you're not using any investigative skill, all you're doing is casting a wide net against one group, one segment of society, and that's what we call "going fishing," and you're going to come up empty-handed. The better way is to simply investigate terrorism by behaviors exhibited by specific individuals. It's not the color of one's skin or their ethnicity that should indict them or bring them under police scrutiny. It should be their behaviors or actions—what they do.

'Right after 9/11 everybody wanted a quick fix.'

Hiram Monserrate was a patrol officer with the New York Police Department for twelve years. Today, he is a prominent member of the New York City Council, where he sits on the Public Safety Committee. Councilman Monserrate also founded the Latino Officers Association. He is an ardent critic of racial profiling by the police, and, like Barbara Markham, he does not believe ethnic profiling is effective as a law enforcement tool. He told the ACLU:

> It's easy to go to an area like Jackson Heights [Queens, New York] searching out South Asian males under the guise of counterterrorism. It's easy to do that. It's also easy to detain lots of innocent people. I think that is neither a good course of action, nor is it the best use of law enforcement resources. The better way is to do the intelligence work and investigation that needs to be done, and be able to identify individuals where there is reasonable suspicion to believe they are in fact engaged in some type of criminal activity, and then go to those individuals and stop them to question them and ultimately detain them. Good police work is not about cutting corners. It's about using resources and being intelligent. Law enforcement going out and engaging in sweeps and random stops really produces very little in quality arrests.

Jerry Sanders was a member of the San Diego Police Department for 26 years, and for the last six of those years he served as the department's chief of police. Chief Sanders was credited with bringing about a dramatic reduction in crime and for building community-police partnerships. He was also the first chief of police to announce that he would begin collecting traffic stops data on a voluntary basis in order to determine whether or not his department's officers were engaging in racial profiling. He told the ACLU:

> One of the things I can remember being up on the bulletin boards at work was a sign that said, "Random patrol

produces random results." If you're doing this randomly, just trying to blanket places, I think you get pretty random results. I don't think you get a high hit rate. Right after 9/11 everybody wanted a quick fix. I was certainly concerned and I wanted things done quickly, too. But it takes time to investigate, to find out who was involved in these things, and good investigative techniques are not always fast. I don't think you get a quick fix by stopping everybody and getting their names, and then trying to figure out what's going on. I think a much more targeted response would be a much better way of doing that without alienating huge parts of the community.

All three police officers also expressed their concern that current counterterrorism practices that rely on ethnic profiling actually compromise public safety. First, such practices lead to the misuse of scarce police resources. Officer Markham explained:

When you're engaged in racial profiling in counterterrorism you're casting a wide net, and then by process of elimination you have to look at every person in that wide net, and you're going to waste a lot of time, manpower and energy.

Wasting Resources

This is an accurate description of the Justice Department's post-9/11 investigation. In April 2003, the Office of the Inspector General [OIG] of the Department of Justice issued a comprehensive 198-page report revealing in detail for the first time the Justice Department's policies, directives, and activities in the wake of the Sept. 11 attacks. Entitled *The September 11 Detainees: A Review of the Treatment of Aliens Held on Immigration Charges in Connection with the Investigation of the September 11 Attacks*, it was based on a year-long investigation that included extensive interviews with federal law enforcement officials and agents, and with some of the detainees. One of the OIG report's findings was that since the attorney general issued a "hold until cleared" policy for all aliens arrested in the 9/11 investigation, law enforcement personnel had to spend time identifying the detainees, investigating their backgrounds and analyzing whatever information came in from the CIA and other agencies. And each of these investigations was so time-consuming that "[t]he FBI cleared less than 3 percent of the September 11 detainees within three weeks of their arrest." The report paints a vivid picture of the time and resources wasted clearing individuals who in large part were "suspicious" only because of their national origin:

> **Ethnic profiling alienates the communities whose cooperation is essential to the gathering of good intelligence.**

[The FBI's] resources were insufficient to permit the group to analyze the CIA information in a more timely manner for a number of reasons. First, according to one of the SSAs (supervisory special agents) assigned to the project, the volume of cases was simply too great. One of the FBI requests to the CIA for information contained the names of 190 detainees. Second, the SSA pointed to many technical difficulties and "growing pains" they faced when they first started in late November 2001 . . . Third, many of the people working on this project were not focused exclusively on this task, due to the many demands on the FBI. Finally, some of the cases required contacting FBI offices overseas or other agencies, which took time, especially because the FBI offices in the Middle Eastern countries also were overburdened at the time.

At a time when every investigator could have been following up real leads based on observation of "pre-attack" behaviors, many were tied to their desks, clearing individuals about whom there was no reason to be suspicious. What's more, the futility of this effort became clear early in the process. According to the report, "A variety of INS [Immigration and Naturalization Service], FBI and Department officials who worked on these September 11 detainee cases told the OIG that it soon became evident that many of the people arrested during the PENTTBOM [Pentagon/Twin Towers Bombings] investigation might not have a nexus to terrorism." But because of the "hold until cleared" policy, the investigators had to go through this futile and time-consuming process.

As was the case with racial profiling during the "war on drugs," ethnic profiling alienates the communities whose cooperation is essential to the gathering of good intelligence. As Police Chief Sanders explained:

> Whole communities get very upset when they see that pretty soon everybody that they love has been arrested, and I think that creates far more problems. The issue is one of community trust. If you're relying on the public to assist you in just about any way, and if you're stopping people in communities of color, and your stops are out of sync with the way they are in every other community because you're simply stopping people because you think they may look suspicious, we found that it's awfully difficult for those communities to support and trust the efforts of what the police are doing.

Councilman Monserrate, whose district is comprised of a section of New York City with a large South Asian population, also commented on this problem:

> I do know that in the South Asian community, there is a lot of concern about people being taken off the street and detained without charge. That leaves an aura of fear and suspicion. And I think that fear and suspicion largely hampers the police mandate to help protect property and lives. The best way is for the communities

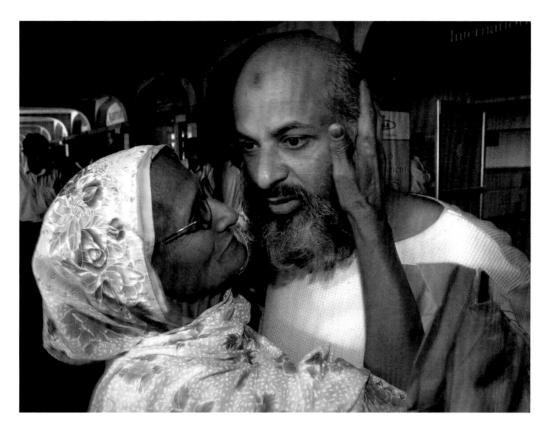

to be partners with the police and not to be in fear of the police, because that hampers public safety.

The Human Costs

The human costs of our government's ethnic profiling policies are incalculable: hardworking, law-abiding men suddenly finding themselves shackled hand and foot, held incommunicado in solitary confinement for months at a time; families separated; homes and businesses lost; and lives turned upside down. For many, the greatest loss of all was the bitter discovery that their adopted country, which promised freedom and opportunity, no longer wanted them.

In November 2002, frustrated by the continuing refusal of the Department of Justice to reveal the identi-

A mistaken perception of Muslims as terrorists means U.S. authorities will investigate, detain, and deport more Muslims. (**AP Images.**)

ties and happenstances of most of the post-9/11 detainees, the ACLU decided to conduct its own investigation. With the assistance of the Human Rights Commission of Pakistan, we located 21 detainees who had been deported to Pakistan, or who had left the U.S. voluntarily to avoid indefinite detention. We met with these men in Lahore, Karachi and Islamabad. Their accounts . . . are a powerful indictment of our government's abuse of power. Justice Thurgood Marshall once wrote:

> Profiling by race, ethnicity, religion or national origins runs counter to what is arguably the core principle of American democracy.

History teaches that grave threats to liberty often come in times of urgency, when constitutional rights seem too extravagant to endure. The World War II camp cases, and the Red Scare and McCarthy-era internal subversion cases, are only the most extreme reminders that when we allow fundamental freedoms to be sacrificed in the name of real or perceived exigency, we invariably come to regret it.

In the post-9/11 era, the treatment of Arabs, Muslims and South Asians can be added to Justice Marshall's list of "extreme reminders." . . .

Core Principles of American Democracy

The practice of profiling by race, ethnicity, religion or national origin runs counter to what is arguably the core principle of American democracy: that humans are created equal, and are entitled to be treated equally by the government, irrespective of immutable characteristics like skin color, faith and ethnic or national origin.

The argument for bias in policing is a self-fulfilling prophecy. If blacks are considered by police to be more likely to commit crimes, they will be stopped and investigated more than whites, and the "crime rate" among blacks will increase. Likewise, if the police concentrated their efforts on white citizens, they would find an increased hit rate among whites as well. If Arabs or Muslims are considered by the Department of Justice more likely to be terrorists, it will investigate, detain, interrogate and deport more Muslims or Arabs, consequently creating a numerical basis for the initial belief.

> "Racial, ethnic, religious or national origin profiling actually poses a national security risk."

Numerous law enforcement officials believe that racial, ethnic, religious or national origin profiling actually poses a national security risk. If you are an airport screener and you believe that every terrorist is going to be Middle Eastern, you are not going to look as hard at people of other ethnicities. In addition, bias-based profiling—because of its lack of specificity—wastes resources and ineffectively allocates personnel.

At stake in the fight to end racial profiling are the fundamental principles of democracy upon which our country is based. Those principles deserve our vigorous protection.

The Air in New York Was Not Safe to Breathe After the Attacks

Andrew Stephen

Despite assurances from the George W. Bush administration, the air in New York following the 9/11 attacks was not fit to breathe, maintains Andrew Stephen in the following viewpoint. The cloud of dust and debris exposed people who lived and worked near Ground Zero to dozens of toxic substances, he asserts. Indeed, Stephen claims, cases of asthma and sarcoidosis, a rare lung condition, have increased among those exposed. In fact, New York's chief medical examiner certified that the death of Felicia Dunn-Jones in 2002 was connected to the dust she breathed as she ran from the area of the collapsing World Trade Center towers. As the number of those claiming to have been exposed climbs, Congress is demanding accountability and is asking for funds to pay for the health care of those most affected. Stephen is the U.S. editor of the *New Statesman*, a British newsmagazine.

SOURCE. Andrew Stephen, "The Poisonous Legacy of 9/11," *New Statesman (50 ideas for Brown's Britain Issue)*, vol. 136, June 4, 2007, pp. 24–26. Copyright © 2007 New Statesman, Ltd. Reproduced by permission.

Itook the train to New York a few days ago [in June 2007]—now definitely the only way to go, given the hellishness of travelling by plane in the US—and found Manhattan pulsating with life, as usual. My taxi driver careened through rush-hour traffic at the customary high speed and even managed to hit a man, who, miraculously, was not hurt. Restaurant workers were noisily picketing their workplaces, protesting at management for keeping large portions of the tips meant for them. The ever-widening gap between rich and poor was more evident than ever—18,000 children aged five or under spend their nights in New York's homeless shelters, while the average yearly salary of a top hedge-fund manager, typically based in this city, has just been calculated at $363m [million].

Settling Insurance Claims

Two fascinating facts emerged during my visit. The first was that the insurance companies have settled the last of the claims arising from the 11 September 2001 New York atrocities, clearing the way for thousands of workers to swarm into the 16-acre pit left by the World Trade Center [WTC] to begin a $9bn [billion] rebuilding project.

The second could ultimately make the $4.55bn paid out by the likes of Swiss Re, Allianz Global Risks and Zurich American seem paltry. With a stroke of his pen, New York's chief medical examiner, Dr Charles Hirsch, certified that the death from sarcoidosis (a relatively rare lung condition) of 42-year-old Felicia Dunn-Jones in 2002 was "with certainty beyond a reasonable doubt" connected with dust she had breathed in as she ran from her office a block away from the twin towers on 11 September. Before my visit to New York, the death toll from the twin towers

> A Chernobyl-type cloud of dust and debris blew and settled not just over Manhattan, but as far afield as Brooklyn and even New Jersey.

attacks stood at 2,749; when I left, it was 2,750, with the death of Dunn-Jones officially labelled a "homicide."

Collateral Damage

This was the first such formal classification of what the [President George W.] Bush administration might call "collateral damage" from the 11 September attacks. A New Jersey pathologist ruled that the death last year from pulmonary fibrosis of 34-year-old James Zadroga, a New York City police detective who had spent hundreds of hours combing through the carnage was, "with a reasonable degree of medical certainty . . . directly related to the 9/11 incident," but this finding has not been accepted by the city authorities.

So are we witnessing the first confirmed details emerging of the most serious of all of the 9/11 cover-ups by the Bush administration, which will make the 2,973 overall deaths seem a vast underestimate? Witnesses to 9/11 (who include my friend Conor O'Clery, the legendary Irish foreign correspondent now retired from the *Irish Times*, who tells me that he breathed in noxious substances for months afterwards) say that a Chernobyl-type cloud of dust and debris blew and settled not just over Manhattan, but as far afield as Brooklyn and even New Jersey, too.

A 9/11 Health Crisis

Indeed, 700,000 people have added their names to a registry of those who believe they were exposed to toxic substances; the actual figure could be smaller, or it could run into millions—10,000 of them so far have filed court claims. A Brooklyn study released last month [in May 2007] found that cases of asthma there alone had increased 2.4 times since 11 September 2001. In the year following the attacks, firefighters developed sarcoidosis at five times the rate they had done so before; 26 firefighters who were working at Ground Zero within 72

The 9/11 terrorist attacks filled New York's air with asbestos and other materials hazardous to human health. (**Jose Jimenez/Primera Hora/ Getty Images.**)

hours of the attack subsequently developed the disease, according to the findings of a study published last month in the medical journal *Chest Physician*.

The American College of Preventive Medicine, meanwhile, has expressed fears that deadly, malignant mesothelioma could develop in those exposed. Scores of rescue workers—40 per cent of whom have no medical insurance—have already developed rare blood-cell cancers and thousands of firefighters have been treated for serious respiratory problems.

"The 9/11 health crisis is an emergency on a national scale, and it requires a federal response," says Carolyn Maloney, Democratic congresswoman from New York, who adds that citizens from all 50 states in the Union as well as foreigners are affected.

> The EPA knew all along that the air hundreds of thousands were breathing was potentially as 'caustic and corrosive as Drano.'

Lies About the Dangers

The scandal is that the Bush administration knew almost immediately of the dangers of the toxic New York air, but lied. The public could breathe free, secure in the knowledge that "it is not being exposed to excessive levels of asbestos or other harmful substances," according to Christine Todd Whitman, the former New Jersey governor appointed by Bush to lead the US Environmental Protection Agency (EPA) in January 2001. Speaking seven days after the attacks, she said: "I am glad to reassure the people of New York . . . that their air is safe to breathe." The then mayor, Rudy Giuliani, chimed in to say that air quality was "safe and acceptable." Both Whitman and Giuliani, subsequent investigations suggest, were under pressure from the White House to provide these reassurances in order to keep Wall Street operating.

In the words of O'Clery, "We were systematically misled." Dr Cate Jenkins, a senior EPA scientist who has kept her job despite accusing Whitman and others of lying, says the EPA knew all along that the air hundreds of thousands were breathing was potentially as "caustic and corrosive as Drano," the best-known American drain declogger.

Dr Marjorie Clarke—an environmental scientist at the City University of New York—likewise contradicted the Bush administration when she warned a Senate committee that, far from it being the case that the air in New York was safe to breathe, the attacks had "produced uncontrolled emissions equivalent to dozens of asbestos factories, incinerators and crematoria, as well as a volcano." These "created an unprecedented quantity and combination of dozens of toxic and carcinogenic substances" and were "dispersed over a large area for several months," including parts of New Jersey. "US Geological Survey aerial maps in late September 2001," she found, "show asbestos contamination in Manhattan miles from the WTC."

> "More than 2,500 . . . contaminants were released into the air on 9/11."

The first 34 floors of the twin towers contained asbestos sprayed on to beams, floors and ceilings as fire retardants. More than 2,500 other contaminants were released into the air on 9/11, including fibreglass, mercury, cadmium, lead, dioxin, crystalline silicon and benzene—substances which, when breathed in, can cause not just cancer, but cardiac, kidney, liver and neurological diseases, besides pulmonary disorders such as asthma. The smaller the particles, the more dangerous they become; Clarke says they can be so microscopic that the natural coughing reflex fails to expel them, leaving them to accumulate on the lungs "for decades."

Cutting Corners

I have always expressed admiration for Giuliani's visible leadership on the streets of New York on 11 September (in contrast with that of Bush, who chose to stay aloft in *Air Force One* rather than return to DC to take command). But Giuliani's subsequent decisions, which restored his then-ailing mayoralty to the extent that he is now a frontrunner for the 2008 Republican presidential nomination, are more questionable. He adopted the galvanising and macho "we'll show 'em" attitude so much in vogue at the time, which resulted in the debris being cleared in nine months, rather than the 30 predicted—but, in doing so, cut corners in a way that may well have disastrous long-term consequences.

By late October that year, for example—long after hope for survivors had been lost and there was no need for frantic scrambling—his administration failed to enforce its ruling that all workers on the site wear face-mask respirators. Only 29 per cent were doing so.

Then Giuliani himself set a terrible example by visiting Ground Zero and not wearing one, in front of countless workers. The clear-up was so rushed that, still today, body parts are being found on rooftops and elsewhere.

A Call for Action

The reclassification of the cause of Felicia Dunn-Jones's death is, therefore, of more than momentous symbolic significance. Politically, the Democratic wolves are already moving in for the kill: least surprisingly, Senator Hillary Clinton of New York is planning to haul Giuliani before a Senate committee to be questioned about his post-11 September decisions. Representative Jerry Nadler (also of New York) and 22 other congressmen and women are asking the Bush administration to divert $282m to be spent on immediate health care for those rescue workers most badly affected. Nadler "absolutely" plans to bring Giuliani before a House committee, too. "Who made decisions, if any, that resulted unnecessarily in a lot of people getting sick?" he asks rhetorically.

Giuliani's successor as mayor of New York, Michael Bloomberg, is another politician involved in the 9/11 aftermath who is considering a presidential bid. He has been trying to play down the Dunn-Jones ruling. "Think of it as though somebody had gotten—had a beam fall on them and it just took a little while for them to succumb to their injury," he stammered out in a lamentable attempt to explain, instead merely cornering his administration into an even more legally dangerous situation.

How Many More?

Now that the insurance wrangles are over (the insurers had insisted that the 11 September attacks comprised one "incident," while the property developer, 75-year-old Larry Silverstein, who took out a $3.21bn, 99-year lease on the WTC site just seven weeks before the attacks, argued that they were two separate events), work will commence with furious haste at Ground Zero. Buildings doomed years ago, such as the Deutsche Bank, have yet to be demolished, but hundreds of workers have been labouring away at a new $2bn railway station and a brand-new 52-storey building, 7 World Trade Center, has been completed.

This means that armies of workers and engineers and architects will once again be converging on the possibly still-contaminated site, this time labouring to put up the flagship Freedom Tower and the other new buildings that will fill the void. Rock anchors (165 of them) have already been grouted 80 feet deep into 120 tonnes of bedrock.

Poor Dunn-Jones, a dynamic civil rights lawyer who worked for the US education department, did not live to see these developments, because she literally suddenly stopped breathing in February 2002 after developing a cough. But, in a tacit acknowledgement of what had killed her, the US department of justice's victim compensation fund awarded her family $2.6m in damages. A spokeswoman for the World Trade Center Memorial Foundation

> Most galling of all for the families of victims . . . is that the Bush administration . . . did not tell the truth . . . when it was known all along that the air in New York was not fit to breathe.

says that Dunn-Jones will be officially listed as a victim on the 9/11 memorial when it opens in 2009.

But how many more names will there be by then? And in the following decade, or two, or three? Conor O'Clery, who watched from his apartment two blocks away as people plunged to their deaths from the twin towers, says he still finds it hard sometimes to get the taste of that noxious white and grey-brown dust out of his mouth and nostrils, even though he now lives in the Irish countryside.

Most galling of all for the families of victims, and the survivors, is that the Bush administration—as well as one of the two leading contenders for the Republican presidential nomination next year—did not tell the truth about their plight, when it was known all along that the air in New York was not fit to breathe.

Answering the 9/11 Conspiracy Theorists

Dominik Cziesche, Hauke Goos, Bernhard Hübner, Ansbert Kneip, and Georg Mascolo

Since the 9/11 attacks, conspiracy theorists have shared their suspicions on the Internet. In the following viewpoint, Dominik Cziesche, Hauke Goos, Bernhard Hübner, Ansbert Kneip, and Georg Mascolo, who write for the German news magazine *Der Spiegel*, debunk these theories. Some believe that the George W. Bush administration hatched the 9/11 plot to garner support for war in Afghanistan and Iraq. These theorists claim that CNN's almost immediate live coverage of the attack is evidence that the government leaked notice of the imminent attack to incite the nation. The authors explain away this theory—CNN obtained immediate footage because it had fixed cameras near the World Trade Center, a favorite news-spot backdrop. Claims that a U.S. cruise missile struck the Pentagon are easily refuted by witnesses who saw a jetliner crash into the building. Nevertheless, as soon as one theory is debunked, another is born, the authors conclude.

Many of the questions posed by 9/11 can be answered more thoroughly and precisely today, allowing quite a few of the conspiracy theories to be debunked.

For example, information made public in the spring of 2006 clearly shows that the fourth hijacked airliner, United's flight 93, was not shot down by U.S. fighter jets, notwithstanding the numerous Internet rumors. At the trial of the suspected terrorist Zacarias Moussaoui, the prosecution played the audiotape from flight UA 93's black box. It is a dramatic recording, but there is no evidence that the plane was shot down.

Suspicious of the Official Version

In this sense, 9/11 is no different from the assassination of John F. Kennedy, the fatal car crash of Princess Diana and Dodi Fayed or—for Germans—the suicide of politician Uwe Barschel. Conspiracy theories abound. Not everyone is willing to swallow the official version of events. Some are convinced that information is being suppressed—they allege cover-ups, secret plots. They seek to implicate the government. They chat away in the blogosphere. And every attempt to refute a theory by analyzing fresh information spawns a new generation of suspicions.

Still, U.S. officials have done their part to abet the conspiracy theorists. Until recently, when they released the entire film, only five still surveillance photographs of the plane hitting the Pentagon were in circulation. At first, the torrents of debris unleashed by the collapsing towers of the World Trade Center were described as harmless. Today, New York doctors are treating patients with pulmonary ailments accompanied by a serious, hitherto unknown type of cough.

> "Demolishing two buildings the size of the Twin Towers would have been a massive undertaking. . . . Could it really have been kept under wraps?"

The substantial amount of new information available now, five years after the attacks, is inviting a re-examination of the events of the day. Some findings merely confirm what we already knew, but add layers of fresh detail. Others shift the focus, including the exact role played by Osama bin Laden. And much is new. . . .

How Was CNN Able to Provide Live Coverage So Quickly?

It took three minutes for the world to be told of the catastrophe unfolding on September 11. Flight AA [American Airlines] 11 rammed the North Tower at 8:46 A.M.; CNN broadcast the first live shots of the burning building as "breaking news" at 8:49 A.M. with the headline "Plane crashes into World Trade Center tower." The footage was shown simultaneously on CNN's 800 international affiliates.

The instant live coverage is easily explained: CNN had installed fixed cameras at various New York landmarks to provide scenery for live stand-up spots. The World Trade Center was a favorite interview backdrop for CNN Financial News, a now-defunct CNN subsidiary. The camera that captured the burning North Tower was located two miles away on the roof of a skyscraper.

Why Did the Towers Fall So Quickly?

The engineers and fire-prevention experts agree on one thing at least: Both towers would have remained standing much longer had the fireproof coating on their frames not been destroyed in the crashes. Whether they would have survived completely remains a matter of debate.

A May 2002 study by the Federal Emergency Management Agency (FEMA) concluded that the towers had been structurally sound, and that the builders could not be held liable for their collapse. In 1973, when the buildings were completed, they were designed to withstand the impact of a Boeing 707. But 28 years later, the two Boeing 767s that hit the towers were traveling at 475 and 590 miles per hour, respectively, generating considerably more kinetic energy than a lone 707.

A 2005 report by the National Institute of Standards and Technology (NIST) blamed the damaged fireproofing for the catastrophe. Fires weakened the steel frame that supported the weight of the building. This caused several sections of flooring to sag. Unable to withstand the weight of the floors, the steel structures first buckled inward and then caved in completely.

Skeptics doubt that the blaze was hot enough to melt steel. They argue that jet fuel burns at a maximum of about 800 degrees Celsius. To melt steel, at least 1,500° C is required. As a consequence, they argue, fire could not have caused the collapse.

But steel doesn't have to melt completely. At 650°C, it loses 50 percent of its tensile strength. At just below 1,000°C, it loses about 90 percent, according to experts. Moreover, specialists believe that flammable materials inside—such as carpets, curtains, furniture and plastics—helped increase the temperature at the top of the towers to almost 1,000°C.

Why Did the South Tower Collapse First?

Although it was hit 17 minutes earlier, the North Tower remained standing for 29 minutes longer than the South Tower—for two reasons. As AA 11 impacted the North Tower 16 stories higher, there was less weight for the frame to support. And AA 11 was also flying more slowly and therefore caused less immediate damage.

Could the Towers Have Been Blown Up?

Some critics still maintain that the Twin Towers could not have collapsed simply as the result of fire damage. They argue that the buildings must have been demolished. Indeed, television pictures do show minor explosions as the structures collapse.

The report issued by the National Institute of Standards and Technology (NIST) offered this explanation: Pieces of the planes sliced open the utility shafts inside the towers, enabling jet fuel to spread throughout the building. Explosions occurred whenever a spark ignited the fuel.

Beyond this, demolishing two buildings the size of the Twin Towers would have been a massive undertaking. With so many people involved, could it really have been kept under wraps? . . .

Were the Flight Data Recorders of the WTC Aircraft Ever Recovered?

The 9/11 Commission Report puts it succinctly: "The CVRs [cockpit voice recorders] and FDRs [flight data recorders] from American 11 and United 175 were not found." Even before the report's release, experts expressed doubts about the recorders' ability to survive the crash into the towers, the ensuing fire, and finally the buildings' collapse. But thanks to statements made by firefighter Nicholas DeMasi, the whereabouts of the flight data recorders remains one of September 11's unresolved mysteries. In his 2003 book, DeMasi claimed he found three of the four black boxes at Ground Zero during October 2001.

DeMasi's assertions gained further credibility in December 2005 when the magazine *CounterPunch* quoted an anonymous source from the National Transportation Safety Board (NTSB): "Off the record, we had the boxes," the source said. "You'd have to get the official word from the FBI as to where they are, but we worked on them here."

Unfortunately, the source's identity remains a secret. But it is unlikely that three of the four black boxes would

> The cruise-missile theory is . . . discredited by the various eyewitnesses who saw a jetliner crash into the Pentagon.

have been found during a single search at a time when the rubble of Ground Zero was still smoldering.

To this day, the FBI and the NTSB deny that the boxes were recovered. . . .

Why Did WTC 7 Collapse?

The 47-story World Trade Center 7 building burned for seven hours beside the rubble of the Twin Towers—before collapsing in just eight seconds at 5:20 P.M.

FEMA's 2002 investigation concluded that WTC 7 had sustained comparatively slight damage prior to caving in. The 9/11 Commission made no mention of WTC 7 in its findings. And when the authorities remain silent or withhold information, rumors are guaranteed. Didn't the structure collapse a little too neatly? Could it have been dynamited?

The collapse of WTC 7 is currently being reviewed by the National Institute of Standards and Technology. Its experts believe that the building suffered far more damage from the plunging towers' rubble than had previously been assumed, particularly on the south side, the upper floors and the southwestern corner.

NIST's experts also attribute the building's ultimate collapse to the unusually heavy load borne by its individual supports. The buckling of a single support could have brought the entire structure down. The institute has found no evidence to suggest that bombs, missiles or explosives caused the building to cave in.

The final report has already been postponed several times. It is now due to be released this year [in 2006; the final report was released in November 2008].

How Did the Plane Fit Through the Hole in the Pentagon?

The hole that the Boeing 757 drilled in the Pentagon's exterior wall was some 10 yards narrower than the airliner's width. Just how credible is the assertion that flight

AA 77 really did crash into the building? And if the damage could not have been caused by a Boeing 757, could a cruise missile have been responsible?

Conspiracy theorists like the Frenchman Thierry Meyssan maintain that a silhouette of the smashed plane should have been visible on the building's façade—an assumption refuted by physicists, who say that the remains of the plane after impact would have acted like a solid object rather than a fluid. Eyewitness accounts

Federal authorities denied rumors that claim the flight recorders from the jets that struck New York were found. (**Stan Honda/ AFP/Getty Images.**)

reveal that part of the right wing came off when the plane struck a huge generator in front of the building. The plane's left wing was smashed by the façade's support pillars.

The cruise-missile theory is also discredited by the various eyewitnesses who saw a jetliner crash into the Pentagon. What is more, the remains of the plane's crew and passengers have been identified.

Another obvious question presents itself: If flight AA 77 didn't smash into the Pentagon, where is it today?

Where Is the Wreckage from Flight AA 77?

Hardly any aircraft parts are visible on photographs of the crash site at the Pentagon—according to skeptics, further evidence that a plane didn't hit the Pentagon.

But eyewitnesses who rushed to the scene reported seeing sections of the aircraft scattered widely throughout the vicinity of the crash. These included the nose, a tire, parts of the landing gear and fuselage, a cockpit seat and even a chunk of the tail with the plane's number on it.

There is no secret about the fate of the wreckage. On September 12, the *Washington Post* reported that a column of 50 FBI agents had marched shoulder-to-shoulder across the south grounds of the Pentagon, "picking up debris and stuffing it into brown bags. The lawn was scattered with chunks of the airplane, some up to four feet across," the newspaper reported.

Both of the plane's black boxes were also recovered. And all but one of the passengers on board flight AA 77 were positively identified—using remains recovered from the scene.

What Is Visible on the Pentagon Videos?

In contrast to the attacks on the WTC, there is no live broadcast footage of the Pentagon crash. Until this spring [of 2006], only five still photographs taken by a nearby security camera had been released. The photos showed only the fireball and not the plane, causing conspiracy theorists to believe that the administration had something to hide. The complete videos were released in May. A still shows an object approaching at high speed; the image is very blurred. Those who continue to believe that the United States attacked its own Defense Department will continue to maintain that the shape is a cruise missile.

> Few of the calls from flight UA 93 were made using cell phones; the majority came from units built into the aircraft's seatbacks.

After the crash, the FBI seized 85 security videos from the area. Legal proceedings to compel the FBI to release the videos are currently under way. It is unlikely that the footage would yield new information anyway as—according to an FBI official—most of the cameras weren't even trained on the Pentagon. She also stated that few cameras had captured images of the building after the attack, and just one had recorded the impact—as allegedly proven by the recently released film.

How Were the Inexperienced Hijacker Pilots Able to Hit the Pentagon?

The World Trade Center was a relatively easy target. Situated on the southern tip of Manhattan, it would have been instantly recognizable on the horizon. While the Pentagon is also a gigantic structure, it is relatively flat. As a result—as the black box has revealed—the pilot first entered Washington's Reagan National Airport as his destination in the plane's onboard computer. Nearly nine minutes before the crash, he switched off the autopilot.

From that point, the hijackers flew the plane manually, using the joystick and thrust control. Because the plane was still too high for a direct run at the Pentagon, they started a 330-degree turn five miles away. This is not difficult to accomplish and took about 2.5 minutes to complete.

It can be assumed that the terrorists were content to hit any part of the building. Their approach was tantamount to a controlled crash landing, a maneuver that can be practiced with any flight simulator software.

How Could the Passengers Make Phone Calls from the Planes?

Ten passengers and two crew members made phone calls from flight UA 93 before the Boeing 757 plunged into a field in Shanksville, Pennsylvania. Given the widespread belief that cell phones are all but useless at heights of over 8,000 feet, rumors were soon circulating that the calls had been faked.

It is difficult but not impossible to use mobile phones at such high altitudes. Numerous factors determine whether connections can be made and maintained. The odds improve when a plane is over a city or transmitter, or—at least with the latest cell phone generations—flying relatively slowly or at low altitude. Older phones with more powerful receivers—used for analog networks—frequently function at altitudes of 45,000 feet. These older models were relatively common in the United States until recently.

In any case, few of the calls from flight UA 93 were made using cell phones; the majority came from units built into the aircraft's seatbacks. . . .

> If [a stock investor] did in fact have advance knowledge of the attacks, why did he or she invest such a small sum?

Why Were There No Bodies, No Wreckage, and No Large Crater from UA 93?

The crater from the crash near Shanksville is remarkably small. Pictures taken at the site revealed little in the way of wreckage or body parts. Even today, the town's mayor is quoted as saying that he didn't see a plane at the crash site.

In reality, UA 93 was smashed to smithereens by the force of the impact. Still, rescuers did find several substantial pieces of wreckage, including sections of the fuselage. Photos of it were submitted as exhibits in Moussaoui's trial. Body parts were also found at the site, and identified using DNA analysis. Eight months after the crash, 125 volunteers conducted a new search of the area, and found additional pieces of wreckage: metal and wiring. They also collected bucketloads of human remains.

For the record, the mayor was misquoted. He had said that there was virtually nothing left of the aircraft; not that there was no evidence of a plane at all. . . .

Did Investors Speculate on the Attacks?

A few days after 9/11, there were indications that advance notice may have existed of the attacks. Some investors seem to have been expecting oil and gold prices to rise, and also purchased "put" options on stock of reinsurers for both American and United airlines (investors buying put options profit if the value of the stock falls). One buyer pocketed nearly $5 million on 4,744 puts on United stock purchased just four days before the attacks.

A closer look at the trading reveals that this was normal speculation. Both airlines had themselves churned out enough bad news to make investors pessimistic about their stock prices. On September 7, American Airlines issued a profit warning. On September 10, Goldman Sachs announced that it was again lowering its earnings forecast for AA. According to the Commission, the ostensibly suspicious purchase that same day of 4,516 put options was primarily due to a recommendation made in an investors' newsletter on September 9.

Apart from that finding, the profits made provide the strongest argument against any insider dealing. If someone did in fact have advance knowledge of the attacks, why did he or she invest such a small sum? . . .

Why Do Doubts Surround the Official Investigations into the Events of 9/11?

For one thing, several major inquiries in the past have only revealed partial truths. Beyond this, major historic events always provide scope for speculation. President John F. Kennedy assassinated by a lone gunman? Impossible! There must be more to it. The 9/11 attacks on the United States? Allegedly perpetrated by a bunch of Arabs with box cutters and rudimentary flight training. According to this logic, President Bush and Vice President [Dick] Cheney exposed America to attack in order to justify the war plans they were hatching. They had missiles fired at the Pentagon, arranged for the World Trade Center to be dynamited, and ordered UA 93 to be shot down. Beyond the fact that most conspiracy theories aren't backed up by the evidence, simple logic can also be used to debunk them. To pull off such a staggering operation, an army of the complicit would be required: pilots, demolition experts, soldiers and air traffic controllers. With so many coconspirators, one of them surely would have talked by now.

> Beyond the fact that most conspiracy theories aren't backed up by the evidence, simple logic can also be used to debunk them.

CHAPTER 3

Personal Narratives of 9/11

The Final Preparations of a 9/11 Terrorist

Mohamed Atta

The following document, translated from Arabic for the *New York Times*, was found in the baggage of Mohamed Atta, the suspected leader of the 9/11 terrorists. The document outlines how the terrorists should prepare for the 9/11 attacks. It begins with instructions for the last night: The terrorists are to purify themselves according to Muslim tradition and read chapters of the Qur'an that give them courage and strengthen their belief in their cause. The second section instructs that on the morning of the attack, as the terrorists make their way to the airport, they should renew their commitment and show no signs of tension. The third section directs the terrorists to pray for victory as they board the plane and subdue their passengers. When the planes reach their targets, the terrorists are directed to welcome death because they will meet again in heaven.

Photo on previous page: The 9/11 terrorist attacks changed the world politically, but they also affected many individuals in ways still being felt. **(Stan Honda/AFP/ Getty Images.)**

SOURCE. Mohamed Atta, "Last Words of a Terrorist," *Observer (Guardian, UK)*, September 30, 2001. Translated by Imad Musa, Capital Communications Group. Copyright Guardian News & Media Ltd. 2001. Reproduced by permission of Guardian News Service, LTD.

The Last Night [On the Last Night]

1) Making an oath to die and renew your intentions. Shave excess hair from the body and wear cologne. Shower.

2) Make sure you know all aspects of the plan well, and expect the response, or a reaction, from the enemy.

3) Read al-Tawba and Anfal [traditional war chapters from the Qur'an] and reflect on their meanings and remember all of the things God has promised for the martyrs.

4) Remind your soul to listen and obey [all divine orders] and remember that you will face decisive situations that might prevent you from 100 per cent obedience, so tame your soul, purify it, convince it, make it understand, and incite it. God said: 'Obey God and His Messenger, and do not fight amongst yourselves or else you will fail. And be patient, for God is with the patient.'

5) Pray during the night and be persistent in asking God to give you victory, control and conquest, and that He may make your task easier and not expose us.

6) Remember God frequently, and the best way to do it is to read the Holy Qur'an, according to all scholars, as far as I know. It is enough for us that it [the Qur'an] are the words of the Creator of the Earth and the plants, the One that you will meet [on the Day of Judgment].

> Remember the words of Almighty God: . . . 'How many small groups beat big groups by the will of God.'

7) Purify your soul from all unclean things. Completely forget something called 'this world' [or 'this life']. The time for play is over and the serious time is upon us.

How much time have we wasted in our lives? Shouldn't we take advantage of these last hours to offer good deeds and obedience?

8) You should feel complete tranquility, because the time between you and your marriage [in heaven] is very short. Afterwards begins the happy life, where God is satisfied with you, and eternal bliss 'in the company of the prophets, the companions, the martyrs and the good people, who are all good company.' Ask God for his mercy and be optimistic, because [the Prophet], peace be upon him, used to prefer optimism in all his affairs.

9) Keep in mind that, if you fall into hardship, how will you act and how will you remain steadfast and remember that you will return to God and remember that anything that happens to you could never be avoided, and what did not happen to you could never have happened to you. This test from Almighty God is to raise your level [levels of heaven] and erase your sins. And be sure that it is a matter of moments, which will then pass, God willing, so blessed are those who win the great reward of God. Almighty God said: 'Did you think you could go to heaven before God knows whom amongst you have fought for Him and are patient?'

10) Remember the words of Almighty God: 'You were looking to the battle before you engaged in it, and now you see it with your own two eyes.' Remember: 'How many small groups beat big groups by the will of God.' And His words: 'If God gives you victory, no one can beat you. And if He betrays you, who can give you victory without Him? So the faithful put their trust in God.'

11) Remind yourself of the supplications and of your brethren and ponder their meanings. (The morning and evening supplications, and the supplications of [enter-

ing] a town, and the [unclear] supplications, and the supplications said before meeting the enemy.)

12) Bless your body with some verses of the Qur'an [done by reading verses into one's hands and then rubbing the hands over whatever is to be blessed], the luggage, clothes, the knife, your personal effects, your ID, passport, and all your papers.

13) Check your weapon before you leave and long before you leave. (You must make your knife sharp and must not discomfort your animal during the slaughter).

14) Tighten your clothes [a reference to making sure his clothes will cover his private parts at all times], since this is the way of the pious generations after the Prophet. They would tighten their clothes before battle. Tighten your shoes well, wear socks so that your feet will be solidly in your shoes. All of these are worldly things [that humans can do to control their fate, although God decrees what will work and what won't] and the rest is left to God, the best One to depend on.

15) Pray the morning prayer in a group and ponder the great rewards of that prayer. Make supplications afterwards, and do not leave your apartment unless you have performed ablution before leaving, because the angels will ask for your forgiveness as long as you are in a state of ablution, and will pray for you. This saying of the Prophet was mentioned by An-Nawawi in his book, *The Best of Supplications*. Read the words of God: 'Did you think that We created you for no reason . . . ' from the Al-Mu'minun Chapter.

The Second Step

When the taxi takes you to (M) [this initial could stand for *matar*, "airport" in Arabic] remember God constantly

while in the car. (Remember the supplication for entering a car, for entering a town, the supplication of place
and other supplications).

When you have reached (M) and have left the taxi,
say a supplication of place ['Oh Lord, I ask you for the
best of this place, and ask you to protect me from its
evils'], and everywhere you go say
that prayer and smile and be calm,
for God is with the believers. And
the angels protect you without you
feeling anything. Say this supplication: 'God is more dear than all of His
creation.' And say: 'Oh Lord, protect
me from them as You wish.' And say:
'Oh Lord, take your anger out on [the
enemy] and we ask You to protect us
from their evils.' And say: 'Oh Lord,
block their vision from in front of them, so that they may
not see.' And say: 'God is all we need, He is the best to
rely upon.' Remember God's words: 'Those to whom the
people said, "The people have gathered to get you, so fear
them," but that only increased their faith and they said,
God is all we need, He is the best to rely upon.' After you
say that, you will find [unclear] as God promised this to
his servants who say this supplication:

1) They will come back [from battle] with God's
blessings

2) They were not harmed

3) And God was satisfied with them.

> Do not seem confused or show signs of nervous tension. Be happy, optimistic, calm because you are heading for a deed that God loves and will accept.

God says: 'They came back with God's blessings, were
not harmed, and God was satisfied with them, and God
is ever-blessing.'

All of their equipment and gates and technology will
not prevent, nor harm, except by God's will. The believers do not fear such things. The only ones that fear it are

the allies of Satan, who are the brothers of the devil. They have become their allies, God save us, for fear is a great form of worship, and the only one worthy of it is God. He is the only one who deserves it. He said in the verses: 'This is only the Devil scaring his allies' who are fascinated with Western civilisation, and have drank the love [of the West] like they drink water [unclear] and have become afraid of their weak equipment, 'so fear them not, and fear Me, if you are believers.'

Fear is a great worship. The allies of God do not offer such worship except for the one God, who controls everything. [Unclear] with total certainty that God will weaken the schemes of non-believers. God said: 'God will weaken the schemes of the non-believers.'

> Give us victory and make the ground shake under their feet.

You must remember your brothers with all respect. No one should notice that you are making the supplication, 'There is no God but God,' because if you say it 1,000 times no one will be able to tell whether you are quiet or remember God. And among its miracles is what the Prophet, peace be upon him, said: 'Whoever says, "There is no God but God," with all his heart, goes to heaven.' The prophet, peace be upon him, said: 'If you put all the worlds and universes on one side of the balance, and "No God but God" on the other, "No God but God" will weigh more heavily.' You can repeat these words confidently, and this is just one of the strengths of these words. Whoever thinks deeply about these words will find that they have no dots [in the Arabic letter] and this is just one of its greatnesses, for words that have dots in them carry less weight than those that do not. And it is enough that these are the words of monotheism, which will make you steadfast in battle [unclear] as the prophet, peace be upon him, and his companions, and those who came after them, God willing, until the Day of Judgment.

A picture of accused hijacker Mohamed Atta hangs in the home of his father. Atta urged his fellow hijackers to "dedicate the slaughter to [their] fathers." (AP Images.)

Do not seem confused or show signs of nervous tension. Be happy, optimistic, calm because you are heading for a deed that God loves and will accept. It will be the day, God willing, you spend with the women of paradise.

[poetry] Smile in the face of hardship young man/ For you are heading toward eternal paradise

You must remember to make supplications wherever you go, and anytime you do anything, and God is with his faithful servants, He will protect them and make their tasks easier, and give them success and control, and victory, and everything . . .

The Third Phase

When you ride the (T) [probably for *tayyara*, aeroplane in Arabic], before your foot steps in it, and before you enter it, you make a prayer and supplications. Remember that this is a battle for the sake of God. As the prophet, peace be upon him, said, 'An action for the sake of God is better than all of what is in this world.' When you step inside the (T), and sit in your seat, begin with the known supplications that we have mentioned before. Be busy with the constant remembrance of God. God said: 'Oh ye faithful, when you find the enemy be steadfast, and remember God constantly so that you may be successful.' When the (T) moves, even slightly, toward (Q) [unknown reference], say the supplication of travel. Because you are traveling to Almighty God, so be attentive on this trip.

Then [unclear] it takes off. This is the moment that both groups come together. So remember God, as He said in His book: 'Oh Lord, pour your patience upon us and make our feet steadfast and give us victory over the infidels.' And His words: 'And the only thing they said Lord, forgive our sins and excesses and make our feet steadfast and give us victory over the infidels.' And His prophet said: 'Oh Lord, You have revealed the book, You move the clouds, You gave us victory over the enemy, conquer them and give us victory over them.' Give us victory and make the ground shake under their feet. Pray for yourself and all your brothers that they may be victorious and hit their targets and ask God to grant you martyrdom facing the enemy, not running away from it, and for Him to grant you patience and the feeling that anything that happens to you is for Him.

> When the confrontation begins, strike like champions who do not want to go back to this world.

Then every one of you should prepare to carry out his role in a way that would satisfy God. You should clench your teeth, as the pious early generations did.

When the confrontation begins, strike like champions who do not want to go back to this world. Shout, '*Allahu Akbar*,' because this strikes fear in the hearts of the non-believers. God said: 'Strike above the neck, and strike at all of their extremities.' Know that the gardens of paradise are waiting for you in all their beauty, and the women of paradise are waiting, calling out, 'Come hither, friend of God.' They have dressed in their most beautiful clothing.

If God decrees that any of you are to slaughter, dedicate the slaughter to your fathers and [unclear], because you have obligations toward them. Do not disagree, and obey. If you slaughter, do not cause the discomfort of those you are killing, because this is one of the practices of the prophet, peace be upon him. On one condition: that you do not become distracted by [unclear] and neglect what is greater, paying attention to the enemy. That would be treason, and would do more damage than good. If this happens, the deed at hand is more important than doing that, because the deed is an obligation, and [the other thing] is optional. And an obligation has priority over an option.

> **Either end your life while praying, seconds before the target, or make your last words: 'There is no God but God, Muhammad is His messenger.'**

Do not seek revenge for yourself. Strike for God's sake. One time Ali bin Abi Talib [a companion and close relative of the prophet Muhammad] fought with a non-believer. The non-believer spit on Ali, may God bless him. Ali [unclear] his sword, but did not strike him. When the battle was over, the companions of the prophet asked him why he had not smitten the non-believer. He said, 'After he spat at me, I was afraid I would be striking at him in revenge for myself, so I lifted my sword.' After he renewed his intentions, he went back and killed the man. This means that before you do anything, make sure your soul is prepared to do everything for God only.

Then implement the way of the prophet in taking prisoners. Take prisoners and kill them. As Almighty

God said: 'No prophet should have prisoners until he has soaked the land with blood. You want the bounties of this world [in exchange for prisoners] and God wants the other world [for you], and God is all-powerful, all-wise.'

If everything goes well, every one of you should pat the other on the shoulder in confidence that (M) and (T) number (K). Remind your brothers that this act is for Almighty God. Do not confuse your brothers or distract them. He should give them glad tidings and make them calm, and remind them [of God] and encourage them. How beautiful it is for one to read God's words, such as: 'And those who prefer the afterlife over this world should fight for the sake of God.' And His words: 'Do not suppose that those who are killed for the sake of God are dead; they are alive . . . ' And others. Or they should sing songs to boost their morale, as the pious first generations did in the throes of battle, to bring calm, tranquillity and joy to the hearts of his brothers.

Do not forget to take a bounty, even if it is a glass of water to quench your thirst or that of your brothers, if possible. When the hour of reality approaches, the zero hour, [unclear] and wholeheartedly welcome death for the sake of God. Always be remembering God. Either end your life while praying, seconds before the target, or make your last words: 'There is no God but God, Muhammad is His messenger'.

Afterwards, we will all meet in the highest heaven, God willing.

If you see the enemy as strong, remember the groups [that had formed a coalition to fight the prophet Muhammad]. They were 10,000. Remember how God gave victory to his faithful servants. He said: 'When the faithful saw the groups, they said, this is what God and the prophet promised, they said the truth. It only increased their faith.'

And may the peace of God be upon the prophet.

In the Eye of the Storm: A New York Journalist's Story

John Bussey

In this firsthand account, John Bussey, a staff reporter for the *Wall Street Journal*, relates his 9/11 experience. The offices of the *Journal* were located across the street from the World Trade Center in New York City. On that fateful morning, Bussey was there to report what he saw after the first plane crashed into the North Tower. His most vivid memory is of the falling bodies of those who chose to leap to their death rather than face the fire. After retreating inside the *Journal* building, Bussey describes the sound of the floors of the South Tower collapsing and his efforts to escape from the resulting smoke and debris. Once outside again, he and other evacuees began to seek refuge when the North Tower collapsed and a nearby fireman yelled for them to run. The fireman led them through the blackness and choking ash until they reached safety.

SOURCE. John Bussey, "Eye of the Storm: One Journey Through Desperation and Chaos," *Wall Street Journal*, September 12, 2001. Copyright © 2001 by Dow Jones. Republished with permission of Wall Street Journal, conveyed through Copyright Clearance Center, Inc.

If there's only one sight I'll remember from the destruction of the World Trade Center, it is the flight of desperation—a headlong leap from the top-most floors by those who chose a different death than the choking smoke and flame. Some fell swinging their arms and legs, looking down as the street came up at them. Others fell on their backs, peering upward toward the flames and sky. They dropped like deadweight, several seconds, hopeless and unhelpable.

And always the same end. Some crashed into the plastic awning over the entrance to the North Tower. Others hit a retaining wall. Still others landed on lamp-posts and shrubbery. After the 80-floor drop, the impact left small puffs of pink and red vapor drifting at ground level. Firefighters arriving on the scene ran for cover.

The Moment of Impact

In the movie *Armageddon*, the asteroids pierced New York buildings, sending shrapnel out the other side. That, remarkably, is exactly what it looked like from the street, when the first plane hit the north tower of the World Trade Center.

The first warning was the sound of jet engines, flying low over the island of Manhattan. A second or two later, what seemed like a sonic boom.

From the sidewalk, behind the building that houses the *Wall Street Journal*'s offices just across the street from the World Trade towers, I didn't see the first plane dive into its target. But I saw the result: an arc of debris, aflame against the blue sky, coughed from the building southward, landing blocks away.

By the time I'd gotten to the ninth floor of the *Journal*'s building and taken a position at a window in the north-east corner, diagonally across an intersection from the World Trade Center, the conflagration was well under-way. Great clouds of smoke pushed skyward. Intense flames were consuming higher floors above the crash site. Debris was falling onto the streets—huge chunks of metal clanged as they hit the earth. Office papers littered the ground. Cars in a nearby parking lot—a full two city blocks from the explosion—were aflame.

Reporting from the Scene

I called our partner, CNBC, the business news television service, and began reporting the scene from inside our offices, beneath the burning structure. Then suddenly—as suddenly as the first explosion—I saw the second tower erupt in flame, sending more debris crashing southward. This time, the television cameras, located in midtown Manhattan and pointed south, caught the image of a commercial jet veering into the second tower.

> One after the other, from top to bottom, with a fraction of a second between, the floors blew to pieces.

Evacuations were emptying buildings on both sides of the street, and fire trucks, Emergency Medical Services [EMS] vehicles and police cars were crowding the area in front of the World Trade Center. Traffic was halted many blocks north and south.

Then, as the fires worsened, and the smoke got blacker and thicker, the first of the office workers began to jump. One at a time, a few seconds apart.

Unknown to the dozens of firefighters on the street, and those of us still in offices in the neighborhood, the South Tower was weakening structurally. Off the phone, and collecting my thoughts for the next report, I heard metallic crashes and looked up out of the office window to see what seemed like perfectly synchronized explosions coming from each floor, spewing glass and metal outward. One after the other, from top to bottom, with a fraction of a second between, the floors blew to pieces. It was the building apparently collapsing in on itself, pancaking to the earth.

Escaping the Smoke and Dust

This was too close. Uncertain whether the building would now fall on ours, I dove under a desk. The windows were pelted by debris, apparently breaking—I'd never know for sure. The room filled with ash, concrete dust, smoke, the detritus of South Tower. It was choking, and as more debris rained down onto and into the building, the light of the day disappeared. I crawled on the floor and braced myself under a desk deeper in the office. But the air was as bad.

With my shirt now over my mouth in the blackout of the smoke, unable to do more than squint because of the stinging ash, and thinking that this is what it must be like on the upper floors of the Towers, I realized I had to move. I stood up from under the desk and began feeling the wall and desks, trying to orient myself in the now pitch-black cubicled world of our modern office. Disoriented, I twice passed by the entryway to this particular corner of the ninth floor. And then I was through, by accident, into a larger space, with more air.

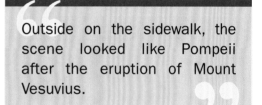

Outside on the sidewalk, the scene looked like Pompeii after the eruption of Mount Vesuvius.

The smoke had spread over the entire floor, which had been evacuated minutes before. In the emergency stairwell, still thinking that it was a matter of time before our building was crushed, I breathed in my first clear air. At ground level, though, it was a different story.

Outside on the sidewalk, the scene looked like Pompeii after the eruption of Mount Vesuvius. Inches of ash on the ground. Smoke and dust clouding the air. My throat stung as I worked my way past ambulances and EMS workers who had been outside when the tower collapsed. The emergency workers were trying to find colleagues. In the silence, as the ash fell like snow, radios crackled: "Steve, Steve, where are you?"

Lifesavers

One fireman bashed through a door of a nearby diner, and a handful of us took refuge from the outside air. We opened the restaurant's cooler, distributed water bottles, and took some outside to give to the ambulances. I asked what had happened to the people evacuated from the *Journal*'s buildings, my colleagues. Did they get away? No one knew.

I stepped into one ambulance with water and asked for a surgical face mask. I was handed several, and later passed them to coughing, spitting emergency workers in the street. The mask would be my life saver.

Because as I walked down the street, getting my bearings, and moving closer to Liberty Street, which opened out onto the Trade Center compound, the second tower was weakening. I heard a pressing metallic roar, like the Chicago El rumbling overhead. And then the fireman next to me shouted: "It's coming down! Run!"

Run where? I had no idea, so I did the best thing at the moment: I ran after the fireman.

Four of his colleagues joined us, plus another civilian or two on the street. We sprinted behind the wall of a nearby apartment building as the North Tower collapsed two blocks away. "Stay away from glass windows" he shouted as we ran, but what he said next was drowned out by the roar passing right through us. We flattened ourselves against a metal doorway, this small group, trying to be one with the building, as chunks of concrete and metal fell from the sky behind us and roared up the street and into the building's courtyard all around us. Debris fell against the shirt on my left shoulder—I couldn't push it any harder against the building.

A Collective Escape

After two minutes, we all went down, in a collective crouch, and tried to breathe. The building had stopped falling. The roar had subsided. But the smoke and ash seemed as dense as tar, far worse than in the building when the first tower fell. We all were wearing the tight-fitting surgical masks which, with shirts pulled up over our faces, made the difference.

Hyperventilating from the sprint and the fear, the group concentrated on not panicking. Our leader, the fireman who warned of the glass, yelled out in the dark: "Is anybody hurt? Try to breathe through your nose!"

> I honestly wondered whether I'd survive long enough for the air to clear.

In the blackness, he tried his radio: "Mike! Mike! Where are you?" No answer. Again, and no answer. My hand was on his trembling back, the better to brace myself, and I thought about asking him how long these blackouts and ash clouds could last. Then I realized the full ridiculousness of the question. How would he know? How often does a 110-story building collapse to the ground? I honestly wondered whether I'd survive long enough for the air to clear.

Mike finally answered the radio and was wearing a respirator. He also had a flashlight. And so eventually he found us. Blinded by the ash in our eyes, we stood up as a line, each put a hand on the shoulder of the guy in front, and let Mike lead us out of the darkness into the lobby of a building 20 steps away.

We poured water into our eyes, and shook ash from our clothing and hair. I looked for Mike to thank him, but he had already left to help an injured EMS worker on the street.

A young man in the lobby, apparently missed in the evacuation, held his daughter, a little blond-haired girl perhaps two years old. She was crying.

An older man who had also sought shelter was raving uncontrollably nearby. We calmed the older man, and the girl stopped crying.

A New York City Firefighter Describes a Day of Horror, Pain and Loss

Robert Reeg

In this firsthand account, 20-year veteran New York Fire Department firefighter Robert Reeg relates his experiences on September 11, 2001, from the sound of the alarm at the Engine Company 44 firehouse to the mourning of lost comrades. Reeg describes the shock and confusion as crowds of people watched the Twin Towers of the World Trade Center burn and the horrific sound of those jumping to their death. When the South Tower exploded, the blast lifted him off his feet and pummeled him with debris that fractured a rib and punctured his lung. While medics ministered to his wounds, the blast that followed the toppling of the second tower battered the ambulance. Reeg tells of his suffering in the ER and his overwhelming sadness at

SOURCE. Robert Reeg, "The Twin Towers Fall," *American History*, vol. 39, 2004, pp. 38–81. Copyright © 2004 Weider History Group. Reproduced by permission.

losing so many fellow firefighters that day. While he eventually returned to work, lung problems plagued him and forced Reeg to retire.

The weather that September in New York was absolutely gorgeous. Cool nights and warm days perked our imaginations for the soon-to-come burst of autumn glory. It was primary day in New York, and voters were lined up outside the school next door to our firehouse waiting for their turns to exercise their democratic duty.

Inside our firehouse we firefighters were preparing for the upcoming day tour. The equipment was being checked, a roll call conducted and the fire engine fueled when the dispatcher's excited voice boomed over the loudspeaker, "A second alarm has been transmitted for Manhattan Box 8087, Number One World Trade Center!"

We all ran to the TV and were horrified by the view of a gaping hole and a mammoth fire burning out of control throughout many upper floors of the North Tower. Speculation ran rampant as the media attempted to determine the cause of this immense fire. With our mouths agape we watched as another airliner slammed into the South Tower and erupted into an enormous fireball. "Oh my God!" I thought. "We must be at war!" In an instant, Rich Boeri, Eddie Kennedy, Matt Shannon and I were jumping on board the fire engine. We knew we'd be responding to the ultimate big one.

Speeding to the Scene

With Eddie behind the wheel and Lieutenant Joseph Patriciello furiously working the air horn, we sped past the voters and headed west. As we turned south on 12th Avenue the hellacious sight of immense fires burning in both towers greeted us. Please bear in mind that in a

> To a firefighter with any time on the job, it was quite apparent that some might lose their lives before the day was done.

high-rise, commercial office building, a one-floor fire is very serious and difficult to extinguish. Furthermore, all the occupants on the fire floor and above are in imminent peril due to the heat and smoke. On a typical business day at least 25,000 people could be expected to enter the World Trade Center. Knowing that, I turned to one of our newer members, Rich Boeri, and commented, "We're going to lose 10,000 people today." Rich just nodded, while continuing to stare, in awe of the job we were responding to.

As Rich stared at the fire, so did the large crowds of people who lined the West Side Highway. They, too, were mesmerized by the magnitude of the drama unfolding before them. Teams of news crews and photojournalists were busy filming us as we donned our masks and shouldered our equipment. Our chauffeur, Eddie Kennedy, who drove the fire engine, hurriedly donned his mask and grabbed an extra air tank. To a firefighter with any time on the job, it was quite apparent that some might lose their lives before the day was done. Eddie could have stayed with the engine, as was protocol, but he chose to join us instead. In a rather poor attempt to lighten a very tense situation I quipped to Ed, "So pal, you're going to join the party?"

"Wouldn't miss it for the world!" Eddie replied.

As Forrest Gump would say, "Had I known what was going to happen, I would have thought of something better to say."

With our gear ready, we headed south toward the command post, each burdened with 100-plus pounds of equipment. From there the firefighting companies would be assigned to operate at specific locations within the fire area. Several times during our trek, both uniformed cops and FBI agents warned, "Be careful guys, the Pentagon's been hit, and there's another plane inbound!"

More than 300 fire-
fighters and paramed-
ics died in the after-
math of the 9/11 ter-
rorist attacks. (**Mario
Tama/Getty Images.**)

The command post was the ramp to an underground
loading dock, chosen to provide a point of refuge in the
event of further attacks. The emotional turmoil experi-
enced by the firefighters in that area will haunt me till
the day I die.

The Horror of Raining Bodies

As we reported in, I noticed one of the senior guys seemingly staring off into space. Unfortunately, it wasn't space he was staring at—it was the jumpers raining down onto the promenade that captured his attention. Boom-boom-boom-ba-boom, the apparent detonations echoed across West Street. Initially I thought bombs were exploding, but then I realized it was the sudden stop following each person's 100-story plunge that caused these gut-wrenching thunderclaps. Looking up, we could plainly see the doomed victims plummeting toward earth. Most of them were running in mid-air, as if desperately attempting to grasp something, anything, to halt their fall to eternity. Their efforts were hopeless, of course, and we felt helpless. Even the saltiest veterans of countless Big Apple fires had never witnessed such a ghastly sight.

A class of "probies" (new firefighters still on probation) had just graduated from the fire academy, and as incredible as it sounds, this would be the first, and last, fire some of them would ever fight. For the younger firefighters, especially the probies, this scene was almost too much for them to bear. I vividly recall one young firefighter's anguish over the ever-increasing numbers of explosions. Every time another person struck the pavement, he would grasp his ears and scream "NOOOOOOOO!" as tears streamed down his bright red cheeks. Another probie was on his knees, vomiting. Several other guys were on their knees with heads bowed in prayer.

The 44th Is Deployed

Then Danny Williams, a well-known and respected lieutenant from Ladder Company 16, took control of the situation. Projecting his most commanding voice, Danny cried out: "Turn around lads, we can't help these people. We must stay focused on our task at hand. Turn around and don't watch them." I think we were all grateful for Danny's orders and readily complied. To this day my heart skips a beat when I hear a loud boom.

One by one the companies were deployed to the South Tower lobby. When the chief called out "44," we began picking up our gear until the chief ordered, "Leave your stuff and go down to Liberty and West and make certain the incoming companies don't block the road."

Eddie argued, "Sure, chief, like they're going to listen to us?"

"I don't have . . . time to argue!" the chief bellowed. "Get it done!"

As we started down to Liberty Street, I noticed a fire department Catholic chaplain. Most NYC fire fighters are Catholic, so after considering the situation, I stopped and begged Father Delendick, "Hey Padre, how's about a general absolution for the lads?" He considered my request for about half a second and began the ritual. I removed my helmet, and he blessed me. Looking over his shoulder, however, I observed another victim cartwheeling down the side of the building. Seeing this, I grasped his arm and corrected myself: "You better make it for everyone." The good Father nodded at me and finished his prayer.

We then headed south toward our assignment. About halfway there, a flight of F-15 fighter jets roared overhead. We all thought this was the third inbound plane— I believe the hair standing up on the back of my neck almost knocked my helmet off.

Upon arriving at West and Liberty, we discovered that the incoming units had not blocked the road, so there was little for us to do. However, about six autos were burning at the base of the south pedestrian bridge. Because the smoke and heat were being drawn into the bridge that crosses West Street and enters the World

> Suddenly I was enveloped by a violent pressure wave of hot air that literally picked me up off my feet and hurled me into the Superman position.

Financial Center, a chief told us to try and knock the car fires down. I went looking for a Purple-K extinguisher, which is very effective on car fires.

The South Tower Explodes

I walked west on Liberty Street a short distance and was in the process of pushing open the roll-up door on a fire engine when I looked up and observed the top of the South Tower exploding. It seemed as if in rapid sequence each floor was blowing outward. My first impression was that a secondary device—either a previously planted bomb in the building or a bomb in the aircraft's cargo compartment—had exploded. No one was near me, so there really wasn't anything to do but run. I had probably put about 50 yards behind me when parts of the building began rocketing past me as if they had been shot out of a cannon. I remember thinking to myself, "This is not good."

Suddenly I was enveloped by a violent pressure wave of hot air that literally picked me up off my feet and hurled me into the Superman position. As I was flying, my helmet was torn off, and a chunk of debris whacked me in the back of my head. I initially thought that my skull was caved in. Then part of the building struck me in the back, just below my right shoulder blade. Usually in the heat of battle a person doesn't feel pain, but instantly the pain was intense. I crashed to the ground and was buried by debris. At this point the air was blindingly thick with choking dust, and it was hauntingly quiet. After all the explosions and the thunderous roar of the collapsing building, now it was as silent as after a new-fallen snow. I remember thinking to myself, "This is it, you're going to die."

> The closest analogy I can draw to being at Ground Zero is that it was like being enveloped in a volcanic eruption.

A Volcanic Eruption

The closest analogy I can draw to being at Ground Zero [the site of the collapse of the World Trade Center's twin towers in New York City] is that it was like being enveloped in a volcanic eruption. Have you ever seen photos of the victims in Pompeii, following the eruption of Mount Vesuvius? Well, that's how I was, curled up in the fetal position, waiting to meet my maker.

I vaguely recall pushing debris and mounds of talcumlike dust off me prior to crawling west. Visibility was zero, and if you could have tied a full vacuum-cleaner bag around your head, it would have been easier to breathe. I'm uncertain how far I dragged myself, but at the time it seemed like a long distance.

When I was at the point where I could go no farther, I bumped head-first into the side of a police van. Reaching up, I found the door handle

> Looking up, I was horrified to witness Number One World Trade Center disintegrate before my very eyes.

and pulled myself in. The air inside the van was clear, and I wondered to myself, "Well, perhaps I will survive after all." And to think that until now I had usually tried to avoid winding up in a police car!

When I had run west on Liberty, the remainder of my company had run south on West Street. Matt Shannon suffered a fractured leg, and Rich Boeri had several head lacerations. Matt and Rich were evacuated to New Jersey for treatment of their injuries. Meanwhile, after about 10 minutes, the air cleared enough so I could see a little. Two emergency service cops found me, gave me some water to rinse my soot-clogged throat and helped me over to the Hudson riverside. At the riverside, several cops and firefighters sat there stunned for a while—we still weren't aware that the entire building had collapsed. I remember thinking that the rest of the Engine 44 members were most likely dead. Captain James "Yak"

Yakimovich, whom I was friendly with when he was a firefighter in Ladder 43, wanted to help me remove my fire gear. I figured that I probably had a few fractures, but there had to be somebody in worse shape than I was, so I told him to go help someone else.

I became alarmed after a cop opened up my firefighting coat, and I was able to feel under my shirt. My chest felt like bubble wrap because a fractured rib had punctured my right lung. Prior to joining the fire department, I had been a New York City EMS [emergency medical services] paramedic, so I immediately recognized that this was a serious condition. At my request, an emergency service cop helped me toward an ambulance until another fire company assisted him. After the medics immobilized my fractured ribs and administered oxygen, the ambulance headed for St. Vincent's Hospital. Just as we were approaching the North Tower, I heard this ominous low-frequency rumble. Looking up, I was horrified to witness Number One World Trade Center disintegrate before my very eyes. Yet another monstrous cloud of volcaniclike smoke and steel was roiling angrily toward the ambulance. "Hold on," one of the medics exclaimed. Seconds later the ambulance was battered by the blast of dust and building parts. Visibility once again became zero, and the road was choked with debris. Fortunately the medics were able to extricate us from that situation and we proceeded on to St. Vincent's Hospital—in a rather hair-raising ride that almost ended in a collision with a city bus at an intersection!

Looking for the Men of Engine 44

Unbeknownst to me at the time, the other members of Engine 44 had survived the collapse. Eddie and Lieutenant Patriciello began running south when they heard the tower starting to collapse. Diving under a car at the last possible instant saved them. There were, however, fires burning over the entire area, and both men were petrified that the car's gas tank would explode. When the air cleared somewhat, they began searching for the rest of us. They found Matt and Rich in short order, and had them evacuated via police launch to New Jersey. Eddie and the lieutenant were very concerned when they couldn't find me. The entire area where they last saw me was buried by incinerated rubble. After frantically searching amid the flaming debris, Eddie cried to Lieutenant Patriciello, "Bobby's dead!" I, too, feared the worst for them as I was "lollygagging" around in the ambulance!

Patriciello was a newly promoted lieutenant who had walked into Engine 44's quarters for the first time about 10 minutes prior to the attacks. He searched for me until he looked like a defeated prizefighter, with his eyes swollen shut from the pulverized glass and concrete. We didn't meet again until we bumped into each other at another fire the following August. When we recognized each other, we just stopped and smiled, and he said quite calmly, "Hey, man, I'm glad you're OK." "Same here," I replied. We both later agreed that if that bellicose chief, who had hollered at Eddie, had ordered Engine 44 into the South Tower's lobby rather than to direct traffic, we probably wouldn't have made it. Neither of us knew if he had survived.

It was a great relief to arrive at St. Vincent's Hospital after a trip that would have made an astronaut vomit. Once inside the emergency room, we found the staff prepared to handle a "mass casualty incident." Unfortunately, there weren't very many seriously injured patients for them to care for. For example, of the 500 or so firefighters operating at the time of the collapse, only about 12 guys were badly injured—343 were dead.

Suffering in the ER

After X-rays were taken, I was lying in the trauma booth when another badly injured victim was wheeled into the

ER. The curtains were closed, so I couldn't see him, but the nauseating stench of burned flesh and jet fuel permeated the air. The poor man's screams of agony were particularly unnerving.

As I lay there on the gurney, I was well aware of what was in store for me. The fractured ribs had perforated my right lung and allowed air and blood to enter the chest cavity. The only remedy for this life-threatening condition is to cut a hole in the chest wall, insert a tube and reinflate the lung with vacuum suction. The surgeons normally do the procedure in an operating room with the patient under anesthesia. But, in a hurry because they were expecting numerous casualties, they just held me down and opened my chest in the ER. It was like having a root canal, sans the Novocain. I wish they had given me a bullet to bite on.

Because I was in a great deal of pain, the doctor later administered a dose of morphine, after which I had several celebrity visitors. Former Mayor Ed Koch, actress Kathleen Turner and Secretary of Health and Human Services Tommy Thompson all came by to see me. As Mr. Thompson was leaving, he offered in all sincerity, "If there's anything you need don't hesitate to ask." I was a bit goofy from the opiates and replied, "Would you consider trading places?" You should have seen the look he gave me!

Mourning Lost Comrades

I'm not quite certain when I became fully aware of how devastating the attack had actually been. The guys in Engine 44 had tap-danced around telling me the bad news. One day a nurse brought me a newspaper in which I saw a list of all the comrades I had lost. On the front page of the *Daily News* was a photo of Tim Stackpole, a very courageous firefighter who had only recently returned to work after recovering from a serious burn injury. He had just been promoted to captain the week before—now he was gone. Mike Lyons, a close friend of mine who had recently transferred to the Bronx from Engine 44, was missing. Mike left a pregnant wife and a 1-year-old behind. I threw the newspaper down in disgust and turned on the TV. The news channel showed the obscene sight of Palestinians celebrating my friends' deaths. That was the worst day for me—it seemed like a bad dream.

But what felt like a bad dream to me was a never-ending nightmare for my brother firefighters and their families. In the hours following the collapse, firefighters continued to respond. One friend of mine compared the Trade Center complex to Dante's Inferno. Destruction was complete, and fires were burning everywhere. Bodies literally sliced in two by falling debris sickened the rescuers as they searched for those who might yet be saved. All the families prayed that their loved ones would be found. Unfortunately, after the first couple of days almost no one was pulled out of "the pile" alive.

> I was never prouder to be a firefighter, and an American, than I have been since 9/11.

The weeks and months following 9/11 were a very difficult time for all of us. For more than a century, FDNY [Fire Department New York] members have been responding to virtually every conceivable type of fire and emergency. Now we had to contend with this unthinkable terrorist attack. Firefighters were concurrently digging at Ground Zero 24/7, staffing the firehouses, trying to help family members of the dead and missing in action, arranging and attending hundreds of funerals and trying to find the time to see their own families. Firefighters, police and EMS agencies outside of New York City were particularly helpful during our time of mourning. Had it not been for the help and support we received from our fellow Americans, I doubt we'd have had the strength to "bear the unbearable sorrow."

Americans Respond

The silver lining behind the black cloud of September 11 was the extraordinary manner in which America responded to New York's needs. Folks from virtually every profession placed their own lives on hold and answered the call for help. Some dug at Ground Zero, while others prepared meals, helped the families of those lost and applied their own professional skills to handle problems that needed to be addressed. My own family, friends (especially FDNY Medical Officer Dr. Charles Dutkowski), neighbors and community helped my wife and kids in every way possible while I was incapacitated. I was never prouder to be a firefighter, and an American, than I have been since 9/11.

We firefighters would like to achieve some form of closure from 9/11, but how can we? Those who were lost must never be forgotten. So how do we move on, but not forget them? Sights, sounds and odors, all of which tend to bring that terrible day back into focus, continually bombard us.

We wish we could see our friends again, but we will not. I wish I could hear Mike Lyons again call out, "44 First-Due!" but I will not. We honor our dead by carrying on the traditions they cherished, as they would have wanted us to. I wish I had a better answer.

A Rookie Police Officer's Courage and Compassion

Nancy Ramos-Williams

Among the first to arrive on the scene, rookie New York City police officer Nancy Ramos-Williams relates her 9/11 experiences in the following firsthand account. She immediately went to work evacuating people from the burning North Tower of the World Trade Center, despite her fears that she was too new at her job to help. When the South Tower collapsed, Ramos-Williams became a victim herself, seeking shelter against the pillars of a nearby building. She describes how a stranger helped inspire her to follow her training and guided her among the bodies and the falling debris to safety. Once back at the precinct, she was grateful that her partners had survived. The experience of that tragic day would forever change her life.

SOURCE. Nancy Ramos-Williams, *Women at Ground Zero*. New York: Alpha Books, 2002. Copyright © 2002 by Susan Hagen and Mary Carouba. Used by permission of Alpha Books, an imprint of Penguin Group (USA) Inc.

I've been a police officer for almost two years, and I'm assigned to the NYPD's Truck Enforcement Unit. We work Lower Manhattan and oversee anything that has to do with truck traffic. Our job is to make sure all trucks comply with city regulations. Before I took the test for police officer and went into the Academy, I worked for the NYPD as a civilian traffic agent for 10 years.

On September 11, I was at police headquarters, maybe 8 or 10 blocks away from the World Trade Center. I'd gone upstairs to do some paperwork, and I was heading to my post with my partners, Richie Vitale and Charles Rubenstrunk. We were waiting for a light when we heard a big explosion. We got out of the van, and we looked around to see what was going on. We saw this huge hole in one of the Twin Towers, and we saw fire. We saw paper coming down, like when we have parades for the Mets.

Guiding WTC Evacuees

So we turned the van around and went through the security system at One Police Plaza, and as we were waiting for the bars to go up, I remember that somebody knocked on my window. I saw this guy trying to show me a badge because he wanted to go down there. I opened the door and said, "Just get in and let's go."

We got there in less than a minute. We parked our van in front of the Millennium Hotel and started running toward Building Five. Everybody from the Tower was coming out through that building.

There were only a few of us there then. Right away I saw two other female officers, Tracy Donahoo and Carol Paukner, so we worked together. We decided to stay near the entrance and help evacuate people. We were telling them, "Run! Get out of here! Don't look back!" We were

> I said to myself, *Oh my God, I'm a rookie. I'm new. I don't have a lot of years on the job.*

telling them to go straight to Broadway, and we told them not to use their cell phones, because they could activate a bomb.

My partners were taking in the people who were hurt or who couldn't walk and helping them to ambulances. I had to stop a few times and help people, because the guys were tied up with so many injured people. I remember helping an Asian woman whose hair was burned to her scalp. It looked like a piece of rug. I grabbed her because she was confused, and I took her to the ambulance.

More people were coming out of the building, and more police officers were coming toward the building. I saw people with no shoes running out of the building. I saw this man walking like a zombie, with no shoes, burned from head to toe. He was very badly burned. There was a lot of blood.

I said to myself, *Oh my God, I'm a rookie. I'm new. I don't have a lot of years on the job, and I'm still learning.* But then I realized, this is the job that I chose to do, and I wanted to stay there and continue helping people.

I remember seeing a man who was blind, and he had a dog. I wanted to help him, but he told me, "No officer, I'm fine. I can find my way out." A lot of people were kind of nasty toward us because we were telling them to run and not to use their cell phones. They were like, "You don't tell me what to do." I thought, *You don't know what's going on. You're cursing me out, but you don't know what is up there.*

Raining Debris

I heard on the radio that there was another plane missing, and they had a feeling it was coming toward the World Trade Center. I ignored that, because I was saying to myself, *These people need me, and I'm going to stay here.* A couple seconds later, I hear a big *Boom!* and felt a shaking. One of the other officers ran toward the street, and I grabbed on and said, "Don't run to the street!

You're going to get killed!" The civilians were running toward the street, and a lot of people were getting killed.

Parts of the building and parts of the plane were coming down, and they were smashing the fire trucks and the ambulances. We ran around to the revolving door of Borders Bookstore, and we could see the orange flames coming at us. It looked like *Star Wars*, because the orange flames were coming so close.

The bookstore was closed, and we were trying to kick the revolving door so that we could get in. We could see all these parts from the building coming down, killing people, and they were falling very close to us. I looked to my left, and I saw the Post Office. I saw this huge chunk of rock hit the wall. There was a delivery guy on a bicycle, and that rock, after it hit that wall, came down in the middle of the street and smashed this guy.

Everything went back to normal, and we could see papers coming down. We were like, "Okay, the first one hit and just paper was coming down, and now the second one hit and papers are coming down again, so it must be safe for us to go back." So we went back to the entrance of Building Five, and we were telling people, "Run! Run!" You could see the fear in people's eyes, and we were seeing more people bleeding and burned.

Seeking Shelter

I felt the ground shaking like an earthquake. Our bodies were going sideways, and I could hear in the background a *Zoom!* like a plane was taking off. I knew that the base of a structure is always support for the whole building, so I ran into the corner of the building to the first column and I just stood right there. People were running into the street, and they were being killed by falling debris. There was a firefighter in front of me, and he was shaking.

I could feel people trying to squeeze me in the back and on the side. I had my weapon on the right side, and I put my hand on my weapon because I didn't want anybody to take it and hurt somebody. I could feel the fire-fighter covering my head with his helmet. Then he kind of cuddled me, and whoever was behind me did the same thing.

My eyes were closed, and that stuff was coming down, and I could feel the air at the same time going *Woooo woooo* and trying to suck me away from the column. I told God, "Just take me if you're going to take me." The air was so strong, trying to suck me out of the area, and I was pushing myself to the wall. I said, "I'm all yours, God, take me," because I didn't know what was going on.

> Our training teaches us that when you're in a situation where you're feeling helpless, you give 120 percent. It's your life. You can't just give up.

"Remember Training"

Then everything got quiet and there was silence. You could hear a pin drop. I opened my eyes, and it was pitch black. I said to myself, *Oh my God, I lost my sight! I can't see! I can't hear anything! I can't see anything! I can't breathe!* I started saying, "I can't breathe!" I felt somebody holding my hand, and he was telling me, "I've got you. Don't worry, I won't let you down." Then he said, "Remember training. Remember training."

What that means is you never give up. Our training teaches us that when you're in a situation where you're feeling helpless, you give 120 percent. It's your life. You can't just give up. You have to continue. That's how I knew he was a police officer. He could have just left me there, and I would have died, because I couldn't breathe.

I was opening my mouth, and the more I was spitting out, the more was coming in. It was choking me, and I couldn't breathe. He told me later that I had been knocked out, and he had given me oxygen. He had a medical bag and he gave me oxygen, and that's when I came back.

So he pulled me up, and we were walking along the building near the bookstore, between the entrance and the revolving door. He was holding my hand as we walked. Then I stepped on a body. I fell onto a headless body, and my hand just let go of his. He looked for me in the debris and held my hands and tried to get me up, but I slipped again. I had hurt my leg, and I couldn't get up.

Looking for an Escape

He told me later that my hand was on top of the person's neck, because it was a headless body. All of the people who stood in that area were killed. They were on top of each other with the debris, and we couldn't walk through there, because when the Tower collapsed, it felt on top of Building Five. We were trapped in the middle.

> I was confused, I wanted to cry, but I couldn't cry, because I'm a police officer.

We made a right turn, and we were facing the back of the church and the cemetery. There was a small gap, and we dragged everybody who was alive out of there through that little hole.

I remember walking, and now I could see, and everything was gray. I could hear somebody saying, "Oh my God, I'm bleeding." I saw this person bleeding from his neck. I saw a telephone on the ground. I saw hands, body parts, and handbags. I saw all that, and I was like, "Oh my God! This is for real!"

I was choking and choking, and I couldn't breathe. He was shaking my shoulders and saying, "Don't give up. Don't give up." He told me that at this point I stopped breathing and that he had to put his fingers down my throat so I could vomit all that stuff out.

I could hear the firefighters breaking into some glass, and they dragged me into a deli. Once I was in the deli, I saw people coughing. I was choking, and the officer who was with me was cleaning my face with water. I knew there were a lot of people around me, and I heard somebody say, "EMS, the officer, her hands are bleeding." I checked my hands. They were covered with a lot of blood, but I was not cut. It was the blood from the body I fell on.

Putting on a Brave Face

Everybody in the deli was dirty, filthy, so I looked at myself in the mirror and I had to clean my nose because I had all that soot. I was confused, I wanted to cry, but I couldn't cry, because I'm a police officer. There were civilians in there, and I couldn't show the civilians that I was shaking. Where were my partners? Whatever happened, I lost them.

There was a lady crying, and I just had to tell her, "You know, it's okay. We're here. Whatever happened, we're alive. You're going to go home to your family. You're going to be okay." I looked toward the door, and I saw so many body parts around the area. As I was getting ready to go out, a firefighter stopped me and said, "Officer, there's nothing for us to do out there. We did our best."

But I was wondering, *Where are my partners? Where's Carol? Where's Tracy?* I still didn't know that the building had collapsed. My chief happened to run into that deli with two lieutenants. He asked me, "Are you okay?" I said, "I'm injured and I can't walk. I don't know if my leg is broken, but I can drag myself." He said, "I want you to drag yourself outside, make a left, go to Broadway, and get out of here. You're going to see some cars out there, and you're going to sit down in one of them."

Helping Others, Helping Myself

So that's what I did. I dragged myself all the way up to Broadway, just dragging one leg. As I was making a left on Broadway, I saw an EMS worker coming out of a building, and she was stumbling from one side to the other.

She said, "Officer, help me! I'm dying!" She could hardly talk. So I grabbed her, and she collapsed in my arms, unconscious. She was very petite and not very heavy, so I held her with my left arm. Then I flagged down one of the ambulances and asked them to take care of her.

I kept walking until I saw one of our Parking Enforcement trucks. My old supervisor from Traffic was inside. I sat down in the truck, and then I saw my chief running toward me. He opened the door, and there was a big mushroom cloud after him. He jumped in the truck, we closed the door, and we were all coughing because a lot of dust came in. It got pitch black. I asked, "What's going on?" and that's when he told me that the second building had collapsed.

> I said, 'There are so many body parts. So many people died down there, and I couldn't do anything for them.'

It got pitch black outside, and we were still there in the truck, in shock.

After it started getting clear again, my chief said, "I'm going to go. Can I use your radio?" I gave him my radio and grabbed a helmet I'd found in the deli and said, "Chief, you might need this." He put on the helmet and left.

The next thing I knew, one of the police officers who works with me came and told me, "I'm here to take you to the hospital." Beakman Hospital is probably five blocks away, and he wanted to carry me, but I said, "No, I can help myself." I dragged myself all the way down there.

When I got to the hospital, they hosed me down with water because I was covered in soot. I was in shock. I know the doctor was asking me a lot of questions. Because I wasn't burned or anything serious, I said, "You can just put something on my leg, give me crutches so that I can walk better, and I'll go to the doctor another day. I know there are people hurt more seriously than I am." We begged one of the ambulances to take us close to our precinct, and we walked the rest of the way. I was on crutches, I didn't have shoes, and my hair was like a pancake because of the soot and the water. I was a total mess. When I walked into the house, an officer looked at me and said, "Oh my God! Are you okay?"

Letting It All Out

My tears started coming down, and I said, "There are so many body parts. So many people died down there, and I couldn't do anything for them. I don't know what happened to Richie or Charles or Carol or Tracy." All this was going through my head, and it was all coming out.

I took a shower, and someone called me and told me that my partners were alive. I went downstairs to the basement, and I saw my partners and Carol, and she was crying. Carol's partner wasn't there, but we found out later that she was safe, too.

When the whole thing was over, Richie told me that when the building collapsed, he said, "Nancy, hold on to my arms." He was thinking that the person he was helping out was me. He said it was pitch black, and when he got outside, he looked back and saw that he didn't have me. He had Carol. He said, "At least I was happy that I had another police officer with me and that we saved each other."

We lost a traffic officer from our division. The guy I picked up, the one who knocked on my window at the beginning, never made it out. He was a volunteer for the ambulance. So inside of me, I still feel guilty that he never made it out. When I'm at my family reunion and there's happiness and joy, I feel sorry that he's not there with his family to do the same thing. That really hit me. I have that right here in my heart.

I'm a Christian woman, and now I appreciate life even more. I've got two kids. Keith is 17, and Nastazia is 10. I still love my job. I just want my life to continue to be happy.

September 11 changed my life a lot. It changed it so much that I got married. Christopher and I were supposed to get married in June, but we kept postponing it. Then with September 11, it got worse, because he's a civilian for the police department and we were both working at Ground Zero. He had crazy hours and I had crazy hours. Finally we said, "Let's do it." And we did.

A Pentagon Search-and-Rescue Worker Connects with a Victim's Family

Rick Newman

Mike Regan, a firefighter and search-and-rescue worker, had never made contact with the families of victims he found until he led a search-and-rescue team through the wreckage left when American Airlines Flight 77 crashed into the Pentagon on 9/11. In the following article, journalist Rick Newman relates the story of how Regan connected with the family of Dan Shanower, a 9/11 victim whose remains he found in the Pentagon wreckage. Regan and his wife have maintained contact with Dan's family, sharing a bond that Newman suggests grew from the ashes.

With instincts honed over years spent working in collapsed buildings, Mike Regan eyed the wrecked innards of the Pentagon for spaces

SOURCE. Rick Newman, "Ties That Truly Bind," *U.S. News & World Report*, vol. 141, September 11, 2006, pp. 41–42. Copyright © 2006 U.S. News & World Report, L.P. All rights reserved. Reprinted with permission.

where victims might be buried. It was Sept. 13, 2001, two days after American Airlines Flight 77 had smashed through the Pentagon's west wall. Regan led an eight-man search-and-rescue team through tangled piles of smashed office equipment. Flash fires flared around them. Finally, the team reached a charred work area. As they began to lift debris, they uncovered a conference table. Then bodies. Some were still sitting in chairs.

Regan approached one of them and coaxed a wallet from the trousers. There was a driver's license that belonged to Dan Shanower, 40, of Naperville, Ill. Regan noted the info on a pad and sent the wallet out to the FBI. Then Regan and his team continued searching. Keep moving, that was the ethos of the rescue squad. Focus on the work. Don't let it become personal.

> Until 9/11, he had never gotten to know a victim or his or her family.

Yet when Regan and his wife, Janice, commemorate the fifth anniversary of the attacks next week [in 2006], it will not be in Virginia, where Regan spent five days combing through the Pentagon rubble. It won't be in New York, either, even though Regan grew up in Brooklyn and lost two close friends, both firefighters, when the twin towers fell. Instead, the Regans will spend Sept. 11, 2006, in Naperville, attending a memorial service in the Chicago suburb and visiting with Dan Shanower's parents, Don and Pat. It's a connection that has grown organically out of the ashes of 9/11. "They have a lot of the same emotions we have," says Regan of the Shanowers. And while seeking solace from the rescuer, the Shanowers have reached out to him, too, exerting a steady, gravitational tug. "It's hard to say no to them," Regan confesses. "We've stayed in touch because of the type of people they are."

It's a new experience for Regan. As a member of Virginia Task Force 1, a group of Fairfax County, Va., firefighters who double as a federal search-and-rescue team, Regan has faced many traumatic scenes: the 1995 Oklahoma City bombing, earthquakes in Turkey and Armenia. Until 9/11, he had never gotten to know a victim or his or her family. But once Regan's work at the Pentagon was finished, he called a firefighter from Naperville he knew, Chuck Wehrli, and said he had found a victim from Naperville. "Dan Shanower?" Wehrli interjected. The Shanowers were well-known, thanks to five active kids and a schoolteacher mom. Dan had been bright, mischievous, and popular. He had joined the Navy after college and become an intelligence officer, bringing home stories of his travels. Wehrli asked Regan if Dan's parents could call him. Despite reservations, Regan said sure.

> After an hour, the Shanowers asked a question the firefighter knew was coming: 'Do you think he suffered?'

So on a Sunday in mid-2002, the Regans' phone rang. Regan and his wife were heading out; Janice was already in the car. When Mike didn't materialize, Janice went back inside. "It's the Shanowers," Mike whispered. Haltingly, Dan's parents asked what Regan had seen at the Pentagon. There were long pauses. After an hour, the Shanowers asked a question the firefighter knew was coming: "Do you think he suffered?"

"I don't think he suffered," Regan answered.

Medals. A 9/11 memorial went up in Naperville in 2003. The Regans were iffy about the Shanowers' invitation to the dedication, but they decided it felt right. Afterward, the Shanowers asked the Regans to their home. Janice noticed pictures of Dan, surrounded by his Navy medals. Thinking of their own three kids, Janice picked up the medals and asked about Dan. "That felt good," recalls Pat Shanower. "A lot of people see the pictures and the medals, but hardly anybody examines or asks about them."

The two families stayed in E-mail contact. They had dinner together when the Shanowers visited their son's grave at Arlington National Cemetery. And now, both sides are looking forward to reconnecting in Naperville for the fifth anniversary. For the Regans, it will be a refreshing moment of solemnity in a world they see growing indifferent to the events of 9/11. "What I like about Naperville is they *have* a memorial to the people who were killed," says Mike Regan. "I live in Herndon [Va.]. People who lived here were killed. And there's no memorial here."

The Shanowers still crave information about their son. If it feels right, they may ask Mike more questions about the Pentagon. And if not, they will still cherish the Regans' presence. "We have a bond with them because they've had an experience we haven't," says Don Shanower. "They recovered our son, and we haven't."

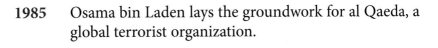

1985   Osama bin Laden lays the groundwork for al Qaeda, a global terrorist organization.

1993   On February 26, using a truck filled with explosives, terrorists bomb the World Trade Center in New York, killing six and injuring more than 1,000.

1995   In June President Bill Clinton issues Presidential Decision Directive 39, which labels terrorism a "potential threat to national security" and vows to use "all appropriate means" to combat it.

1996   On June 25, an attack on Khobar Towers, a U.S. Air Force residential complex in Saudi Arabia, kills 19 service members.

1998   On February 23 Bin Laden and Ayman al-Zawahirir call for followers to kill Americans and their allies worldwide.

In April the Taliban government in Afghanistan refuses to turn Bin Laden over to the United States.

In May President Clinton, in Presidential Decision Directive 62, outlines his counterterrorism strategy and names Richard A. Clarke the nation's first national director for counterterrorism.

On August 7 U.S. embassies in Kenya and Tanzania are bombed, killing 224 people, including 12 Americans.

On August 20 President Clinton orders a cruise missile strike that hits an al Qaeda base in Afghanistan but fails to kill Bin Laden.

1999   In July President Clinton imposes sanctions on the Taliban in Afghanistan for their support of Bin Laden.

2000   In January, an al Qaeda summit is held in Malaysia, following which followers head to the United States to train in flight schools. The CIA tracks two of the 9/11 hijackers who attended this meeting into the United States. The CIA and FBI later dispute whether the FBI was informed of their entrance into the country and fail to explain why the terrorists were not put on a watch list.

On October 12 an attack linked to al Qaeda on the USS *Cole* kills 17 sailors. Strikes against al Qaeda were readied but not ordered.

2001   President George W. Bush takes office. National security advisor Condoleezza Rice retains Richard A. Clarke, but he reports to lower-level officials.

In the summer Clarke and CIA director George J. Tenet express concern over increased terrorist threat reporting.

In June a draft presidential directive calls for contingency military plans against al Qaeda and The Taliban.

In July an internal FBI memo urges scrutiny of attendance at civil aviation schools by individuals who may be affiliated with terrorist organizations.

On August 6 President Bush receives a Presidential Daily Brief warning that Bin Laden is determined to strike in the United States. The brief includes interest in using hijacking. There was no immediate follow-up to this document.

On September 10, 2001, White House deputies agree upon a three-phase strategy in Afghanistan.

September 11, 2001   At 8:46 A.M. a hijacked passenger jet—American Airlines Flight 11 out of Boston, Massachusetts—crashes into the North Tower of the World Trade Center in New York City.

At 9:03 A.M., a second hijacked passenger jet—United Airlines Flight 175 out of Boston, Massachusetts—crashes into the south tower of the World Center.

At 9:06 A.M. the Federal Aviation Administration (FAA) bans takeoffs of all flights bound to or though the airspace of New York, Boston, Cleveland, and Washington, DC.

At 9:13 A.M. F-15 fighters from Otis Air Force base leave military airspace near Long Island, bound for Manhattan.

At 9:21 A.M. the Port Authority of New York and New Jersey closes all bridges and tunnels.

At 9:30 A.M. President Bush, speaking from Sarasota, Florida, says the country has suffered an "apparent terrorist attack." The Federal Aviation Administration shuts down all New York City area airports.

At 9:43 A.M. American Airlines Flight 77 crashes into the Pentagon.

At 10:05 A.M., the south tower of the World Trade Center collapses.

At 10:10 A.M. United Airlines flight 93 crashes in Somerset County, Pennsylvania.

At 10:24 A.M. the FAA diverts to Canada all inbound transatlantic aircraft flying to the United States.

At 10:28 A.M. the north tower of the World Trade Center collapses.

At 11:02 A.M. New York City mayor Rudolph Giuliani orders an evacuation of the area south of Ground Zero.

At 1:04 P.M. President Bush, speaking from Barksdale Air Force Base in Louisiana, assures the nation that all appropriate security measures are being taking. He says, "Make no mistake, the United States will hunt down and punish those responsible for these cowardly acts."

At 4 P.M. U.S. officials say that there are good indications that Saudi militant Osama bin Laden is involved in the attacks.

At 5:20 P.M. the 47-story Building 7 of the World Trade Center complex collapses.

At 6:54 P.M. President Bush arrives back at the White House.

At 7:45 P.M. the New York Police Department says that at least 78 officers are missing and that as many as half of the first 400 firefighters on the scene were killed.

At 8:30 P.M. President Bush addresses the nation: "These acts shattered steel, but they cannot dent the steel of American resolve." He says that the United States will make no distinction between the terrorists who committed the acts and those who harbor them.

At 9:57 P.M. mayor Giuliani says no more volunteers are needed for the evening's rescue efforts. He says that health department tests show there are no airborne chemical agents about which to worry.

September 12, 2001 The North Atlantic Treaty Organization, an organiza tion of North American and European nations, declares an attack against one nation to be an attack against all.

September 18, 2001 Afghanistan's Taliban regime refuses to hand Bin Laden over to the United States.

September 20, 2001 President Bush addresses Congress. British prime minister Tony Blair meets with Bush and offers total support in the war against terrorism.

September 24, 2001 More than 350 people have been detained in the 9/11 investigation.

October 7, 2001 The United States and Britain launch air strikes against terrorist bases and Taliban air defenses in Afghanistan. Bin Laden urges Muslims everywhere to fight the United States.

October 8, 2001 U.S. president Bush creates the Office of Homeland Security and swears in former Pennsylvania Governor Tom Ridge as director.

October 26, 2001 President Bush signs the USA Patriot Act, which grants law enforcement broad powers to fight terrorism.

October– December 2001 During October and through December, a coalition of forces led by the United States ousts the Taliban regime in Afghanistan.

2002 On February 10 civil-rights lawyer Felicia Dunn-Jones dies of lung disease connected with the dust she breathed as she ran from her office a block away from the World Trade Center on 9/11.

On April 15 Bin Laden and Ayman al-Zawahiri praise the 9/11 attacks in a videotape on Al Jazeera network.

2003   On March 1 Khalid Shaikh Mohammed, who masterminded the 9/11 plot, is arrested in Pakistan.

In July the U.S. Congress begins to challenge the constitutionality of elements of the USA Patriot Act.

2004   In July the National Commission on Terrorist Attacks Upon the United States, also known as the 9/11 Commission, faults the Clinton and Bush administrations, the CIA, FBI, and other agencies for pre-9/11 lapses.

2007   In June 2007, New York City's chief medical examiner ruled the lung disease death of Felicia Dunn-Jones a homicide, adding her name to the list of 9/11 victims. Other lung disease victims have since been added to this list.

2009   U.S. president Barack Obama takes office and orders continued rocket and missile attacks on al Qaeda sites in Pakistan.

FOR FURTHER READING

Books

Anny Bakalian and Mehdi Bozorgmehr, *Backlash 9/11: Middle Eastern and Muslim Americans Respond.* Berkeley, CA: University of California Press, 2009.

Lisa Beamer, *Let's Roll: Ordinary People, Extraordinary Courage.* Waterville, ME: Wheeler, 2003.

Daniel Benjamin and Steven Simon, *The Age of Sacred Terror.* New York: Random House, 2002.

Richard Bernstein and the staff of the *New York Times, Out of the Blue: The Story of September 11, 2001, from Jihad to Ground Zero.* New York: Times Books, 2002.

Giovanna Bono, ed., *The Impact of 9/11 on European Foreign and Security Policy.* Brussels [Belgium]: VUB [Brussels University] Press, 2006.

Richard A. Clarke, *Against All Enemies: Inside America's War on Terror.* New York: Free Press, 2004.

Der Spiegel, Inside 9-11: What Really Happened. New York: St. Martin's, 2002.

Louise Fisher, *The Constitution and 9/11: Recurring Threats to America's Freedoms.* Lawrence, KS: University Press of Kansas, 2008.

Stephen F. Flynn, *America the Vulnerable: How Our Government Is Failing to Protect Us from Terrorism.* New York: Harper Collins, 2004.

Nancy Foner, ed., *Wounded City: The Social Impact of 9/11.* New York: Russell Sage Foundation, 2005.

Susan Hawthorne and Bronwyn Winter, eds., *After Shock: September 11, 2001: Global Feminist Perspectives.* Vancouver, B.C., Canada: Raincoast Books, 2003.

David Holloway, *9/11 and the War on Terror*. Edinburgh, UK: Edinburgh University Press, 2008.

Amaney Jamal and Nadine Naber, eds., *Race and Arab Americans Before and After 9/11: From Invisible Citizens to Visible Subjects*. Syracuse, NY: Syracuse University Press, 2008.

Mitchel Levitas, et al., eds., *A Nation Challenged: A Visual History of 9/11 and Its Aftermath*. New York: Times/Callaway, 2002.

John Mueller, *Overblown: How Politicians and the Terrorism Industry Inflate National Security Threats and Why We Believe Them*. New York: Free Press, 2006.

Timothy Naftali, *Blind Spot: The Secret History of American Counterterrorism*. New York: Basic Books, 2005.

Tomasz Pludowski, ed., *How the World's News Media Reacted to 9/11: Essays from Around the Globe*. Spokane, WA: Marquette, 2007.

Gerald L. Posner, *Why America Slept: The Failure to Prevent 9/11*. New York: Random House, 2003.

James Ridgeway, *The 5 Unanswered Questions About 9/11: What the 9/11 Commission Report Failed to Tell Us*. New York: Seven Stories, 2005.

Mark Riebling, *Wedge: The Secret War Between the FBI and CIA*. New York: Touchstone, 2002.

Bruce Riedel, *The Search for Al Qaeda: Its Leadership, Ideology, and Future*. Washington, DC: Brookings Institution, 2008.

Marc Sageman, *Leaderless Jihad: Terror Networks in the 21st Century*. Philadelphia: University of Pennsylvania, 2008.

Bill Sammon, *Fighting Back: The War on Terrorism from Inside the Bush White House*. Washington, DC: Regnery, 2003.

Giorgio Shani, Makoto Sato, and Mustapha Kamal Pasha, eds., *Protecting Human Security in a Post 9/11 World: Critical and Global Insights*. New York: Palgrave Macmillan, 2007.

Cathy Trost and Alicia C. Shepard, *Running Toward Danger: Stories Behind the Breaking News of 9/11*. Lanham, MD: Rowman & Littlefield, 2002.

Paul Zarembka, ed., *The Hidden History of 9-11-2001*. Oxford [England]: Elsevier JAI, 2006.

Amy B. Zegart, *Spying Blind: The CIA, the FBI, and the Origins of 9/11*. Princeton, NJ: Princeton University Press, 2007.

Periodicals

Mark D. Agrast, "Defending Liberty and the Rule of Law After September 11," *Human Rights*, Winter 2007.

Max Boot, "Are We Winning the War on Terror?" *Commentary*, July/August 2008.

David Cole and Jules Lobel, "Why We're Losing the War on Terror," *Nation*, September 24, 2007.

Edward H. Crane, "9/11 and the Struggle for Liberty," *Washington Post*, December 21, 2001.

Ian Frazier, "The Mornings After: Looking Out from New Jersey, the View of the Manhattan Skyline—and the World Beyond—Has Been Changed Forever," *Mother Jones*, January/February 2002.

Laurie Garrett, "Under the Plume: September 11 Produced a New Kind of Pollution, and No One Knows What to Do About It," *American Prospect*, October 21, 2002.

Dwonna Goldstone, "An African American Professor Reflects on What 9/11 Meant for African Americans, and Herself," *Journal of American Culture*, March 2005.

Siobhan Gorman, "Second-Class Security," *National Journal*, May 1, 2004.

Daniel Griswold, "Don't Blame Immigrants for Terrorism," The Cato Institute, October 23, 2001.

Ted Gup, "The Failures of U.S. Intelligence," *Village Voice*, April 14, 2004.

Philip G. Henderson, "Intelligence Failures of 9/11," *World & I*, December 2002.

Andrew Holleran, "The Face of Atta," *The Gay & Lesbian Review Worldwide*, January/February 2002.

Kenneth Jost, "Re-examining 9/11," *CQ Researcher*, June 4, 2004.

Tom Kando, "September 11: America and the World," *International Journal on World Peace*, December 2001.

N.R. Kleinfeld, "Hijacked Jets Destroy Twin Towers and Hit Pentagon in Day of Terror," *New York Times*, September 12, 2001.

Carie Lemack, "The Journey to September 12th: A 9/11 Victim's Experiences with the Press, the President and Congress," *Studies in Conflict & Terrorism*, 2007.

Timothy Lynch, "Hanging on to Liberty in a Post-Sept. 11 World," *Argus*, September 10, 2002.

Gordon MacDonald, "Ground Zero Diaries," *Christianity Today*, January/February 2002.

Andrew C. McCarthy, "The Intelligence Mess: How It Happened, What to Do About It," *Commentary*, April 2004.

Mark Moring, "The Nightmare of September 11," *Campus Life*, January 2002.

Brigitte Nacos, "Terrorism, the Mass Media, and the Events of 9-11," *Phi Kappa Phi Forum*, Spring 2002.

Popular Mechanics, "The World Trade Center (9/11 Myths Debunked)," March 2005.

Sharon R. Reddick, "Point: The Case for Profiling," *International Social Science Review*, Fall/Winter 2004.

Matthew Rothschild, "Who's to Blame for September 11?" *Progressive*, September 2004.

Michael Scardaville, "The Cost of Securing the Homeland," *World & I*, August 2003.

Jonathan Schell, "Letter from Ground Zero: A Chain Reaction," *Nation*, December 24, 2001.

Dennis Smith, "A Firefighter's Story," *New York Times*, September 14, 2001.

Michael Stern, "Attacked From All Sides (Impact of Counterterrorism Measures on American Democracy)," *American Lawyer*, February 2004.

Beth Elise Whitaker, "Exporting the Patriot Act? Democracy and the 'War on Terror' in the Third World," *Third World Quarterly*, July 2007.

Web Sites

National Commission on Terrorist Attacks Upon the United States (http://govinfo.library.unt.edu/911/report/index.htm). Members of the commission, more commonly known as the 9/11 Commission, were chartered to prepare an account of the circumstances surrounding the September 11, 2001, terrorist attacks, including preparedness for and the immediate response to the attack. The commission was also asked to provide recommendations designed to guard against future attacks. The Web site publishes transcripts of the hearings, staff statements, and its final report.

Public Broadcasting System—FRONTLINE (www.pbs.org/ wgbh/pages/frontline/shows/network). This PBS Web site publishes material from its *FRONTLINE* episode "Inside the Terror Network." Based on interviews, correspondent Hedrick Smith explores the personal histories of the terrorist leaders and traces their movements leading up to 9/11.

Neverforget911.org (http://neverforget911.org). This Web site, honoring the 9/11 victims, provides lists of those who died, conspiracy theories and the government response, quotes, a photo gallery, statistics, a timeline, and video footage of the tragedy.

INDEX